AF651858

MENTAL RETARDATION IN INDIA

CONCEPTS IN COMMUNICATION INFORMATICS & LIBRARIANSHIP (CICIL)

For a list of titles in this series
please see pp. 184-187 at the end of the book

About the Authors

VENKATESAN, S., (*b*. 1961) is currently working as Research Officer in Department of Clinical Psychology at National Institute for the Mentally Handicapped, Manovikasnagar Secunderabad: 500 009, Andhra Pradesh, India. After obtaining his post-graduate degree in Psychology in 1985, he underwent two years training in Clinical Psychology at National Institute of Mental Health and Neuro Sciences, Bangalore, wherein he passed his M Phil in Medical and Social Psychology in 1987. He has also passed the membership examination of the Society for Advanced Studies in Medical Sciences, New Delhi, in 1989, with Psychiatry as the main subject. He was admitted to the degree of Doctor of Philosophy from Osmania University for his work on "Analysis of Neuropsychological Function in a Group of Mentally Handicapped Adults".

Over the past nine years, he has been actively involved in the assessment, diagnosis and treatment/training of individuals with psychological problems, disability and impairments. He has over 20 research publications in reputed Indian as well foreign journals. He has co-authored two books, viz, *Behavioural Assessment Scales for Indian Children with Mental Retardation* and *Behavioural Approach in Training Mentally Retarded Children : A Manual for Teachers* in English and Hindi. He has also conducted over 40 workshops in related topics for various target groups, such as, parents, teachers, administrators, etc. Besides, he is actively engaged in teaching undergraduate and graduate students specialising in the field of disability and impariments.

VEPURI, V.G.D., (*b*. 1961) is presently working as Project Coordinator in Sweekaar, Rehabilitation Institute for Handicapped, Upkaar Circle, Picket, Secunderabad-500 003, Andhra Pradesh, India. He graduated from the Officers Defence Academy, Madras, in 1985, and was Commissioned into the Corps of Engineers of the Indian Army. During his tenure in services, he completed his post-graduation in Psychology in 1989. He holds a Diploma in Computers and had an extensive hands on training on Computers. After serving for five years in the Army he left the service as Captain in 1990. Presently he has plans to study in the interdisciplinary field computers and psychology.

In the span of past three years, he has been actively involved in parent counselling, documentation and information processisng, project planning and implementation, research in the field of disability and impairments. His specific area of interest is to develop Computer Aided Instruction (CAI), software for personse with disability and impairments. He has 6 research publications in reputed Indian and foreign journals. He has also translated a book, titled *Management of Behaviour Problems in Children with Mental Handicap*, into Telugu and was published by Orient Longman Limited, Hyderabad.

Concepts in Communication
Informatics & Librarianship 66

General Editor: **S.P. Agrawal**

MENTAL RETARDATION IN INDIA
(A BIBLIOGRAPHY)

S. VENKATESAN
Research Officer
Department of Clinical Psychology
National Inst. for the Mentally Handicapped
Secundrabad, A.P.

V.G.D. VEPURI
Project Coordinator
Sweekar
Rehabilitation Inst. for Handicapped
Secundrabad, A.P.

CONCEPT PUBLISHING COMPANY PVT. LTD.
NEW DELHI-110059

© Authors

All rights reserved. No part of this work may be reproduced, stored, adapted, or transmitted in any form or by any means, electronic, mechanical, photocopying, micro-filming recording or otherwise, or translated in any language, without the prior written permission of the copyright owner and the publisher. The book is sold subject to the condition that it shall not, by way of trade or otherwise, be lent, resold, hired out, or otherwise circulated without the prior publisher's written consent in any form of binding or cover other than that in which it is published.

The views and opinions expressed in this book are editor(s) own and the facts reported by him/her have been verified to the extent possible, and the publishers are not in any way liable for the same.

ISBN: 978-81-7022-546-1

First Published 1995

Published and Printed by

Concept
Since 1974

Concept Publishing Company Pvt. Ltd.
A/15-16, Commercial Block, Mohan Garden,
New Delhi-110059 (India)
T: 91-11-41101460
E: publishing@conceptpub.com, *W*: www.conceptpub.com

GENERAL EDITOR'S INTRODUCTION

In the post-Independence period our social and medical scientists began to take interest in the mentally retarded persons who were hitherto the most neglected lot condemned as unfortunate persons for whom nothing could be done. In the past, it was commonly held that since human abilities are inborn characteristics of the people and since the mentally deficient are devoid of even so much intelligence as to meet their own elementary needs, any efforts to improve their conditions would be futile. But things have now changed. It is recognized that the heredity does play an important part in mental retardation and that through sustained efforts and favourable environment, mental impairments can be improved. It is why the psychologists and educationists are engaged in researches which may lead to the ways to help mentally retarded to be integrated with the society. The feeble-mindness of the mentally retarded may create problems for them, but if they are given proper guidance and are nursed with care they can lead an independent and normal life.

The psychologists and social and medical scientists of the West have made significant contributions in the field of mental disabilities and deficiencies. Their researches are of far reaching nature which changed the scenario of their field. But the researches done abroad, although providing broad guidelines and useful information to our scentists are not very much helpful to them. Since these findings of the foreign researchers have limited value and relevance to our problems if only because the conditions prevailing in developing countries differ widely from those of the developed ones. It is therefore, gratifying that Indian researchers and specialists, who are working under a number of constraints including, in particular the resource constraint, have done remarkable job in their field.

Whereas the Western scientists have flow of funds and at-hand-availability of the reliable reference tools like Psychological Abstracts, MEDLARS, ERIC, Index Medics, etc., providing on-line information in regard to researches of their interest, their counterparts in India not only face funding bottlenecks, but also of easy accessibility to the latest development in their research-subjects and as such have to spend much of their energy and time in locating the relevant information. Side-by-side they live in constant dread of some one else already making investigation on their research topic.

The present publication in CICIL series attempt to provide a reliable reference guide in the field of mental disabilities and deficiences. Besides its concentration on collection of research titles on mental retardation, information of general nature related to their field, such as child development, epilepsies, conduct disorders, mental illness, etc., alongwith their field has also been provided for the benefit of research scholars. It is a commendable job of bringing a large number of articles and research papers published in over 100 Indian journals under bibliographical control which will certainly prove a boon to the researchers in India for whom, in the absence of a good reference tool, the literature search was an exasperating job. The information on Indian researches will also be helpful to foreign researches who engage in studying transcultural aspects of handicapping conditions.

S.P. Agrawal

FOREWORD

In the evolution of any movement it is possible to identify land-marks and turning points that have created history. The developments that have occurred in the field of mental retardation in India are no exception to this. Much of what has happened in this area has taken place during the past fifty years. The adaptation of Binet's test by Kamat, in the late 30s, has been an initial starting point. The founding of the Children's Aid Society and the starting of a facility, in her home with two mentally retarded children, by Mrs. Jai Vakeel in the early 40s is noteworthy. Though inadequate for a country of the size of India, from this small beginning the number of care facilities in the country has now gone up to 700.

The establishment of the All India Association on Mental Retardation (1965) and the formation of the Federation for the Welfare of the Mentally Retarded (India) (1966) brought together individuals from different parts of the country to work together for a common cause. The tradition of observing 8th December as the National Day for the mentally handicapped persons and the issue of a special postal stamp and a first day cover on this day in 1974 by the P&T department has gone a long way in generating public awareness regarding mental retardation. The creation of national awards by the Government of India for the outstanding institutions for the handicapped persons as also for the employers of individuals with disability fortified this process, while the observance of the year 1981 as the International Year of Disabled Persons provided further impetus to this. For the sharing of common concerns and interact, the holding of an All India seminar on mental retardation in 1965 followed by the first All India Conference on mental retardation the next were the beginning. The holding of the 4th Asian Congress on Mental Retardation in India in 1977 and the 7th World Congress of the IASSMD in 1985 were the logical and beneficial development of this process.

When hardly anything was known about the prevalence rate of mental retardation in India, the surveys carried out in 1968 on the school children at Mysore by Kuppuswamy and on a large segment of general population at Nagpur by Varma provided the initial data. The clinical case analysis of 320 cases carried out by Prabhu in 1967 brought out the felt needs and the help seeking behaviour of families with a mentally retarded child.

The establishment of the Rehabilitation Council of India in 1986 as a registered society and its conversion in 1992 into a statutory body by an act of Parliament has gone a long way for quality control in the area of personnel development to work in the field of disability. A new dimension in the care of the disabled individuals, was added with the launching of the pilot project on District Rehabilitation Centre Scheme and the acceptance of the philosophy of community based rehabilitation of disabled persons. A commitment to the philosophy of community based rehabilitation was first heard in this country in the inaugural address delivered by Late Smt. Indira Gandhi in 1966 to the First All India Conference on Mental Retardation Later, during her tenure as the prime minister much of what she said came to be an action plan thus showing her political will and commitment for the welfare of the retarded individuals.

In the recent past, efforts to draft a national policy for the welfare of mentally retarded individuals; form a National Trust; efforts at making adequate provisions for safeguarding the legal and human rights of the disabled persons and the setting up of a National Council for Handicapped Welfare have been the high points.

In the field of mental retardation scattered research has been going on in India since the late 20s during which time Prof. Rice from Lahore (now in Pakistan) worked on the Binet scale. During the early 30s Chand and Choelo published clinical case reports abroad on Down's Syndrome. In the third volume of Ellis' *International Review of Research on Mental Retardation,* Das did a review of research studies available from this country by the sixties. This was followed a few years later by Sen when he did, in the 8th volume of the same series, a review of the experimental, research done in India in the area of mental retardation. The following year, in the *Indian Journal of Mental Retardation,* Agrawal attempted an overview of mental retardation research in India. For the 9th volume of Wortis' annual review of research, Prabhu contributed a review of the available facilities for the care of the mentally handicapped persons. In the mid-80s, an annotated bibliography of available research work on mental retardation was carried out by Prabhu on behalf of the Ministry of Social Welfare. But this report is available only as a mimiographed document.

The current pioneering work undertaken by Drs Venkatesan and Vepuri is praiseworthy. To date this happens to be the most extensive and comprehensive effort in this area As pointed out by them, research in the area of mental retardation in India is still in a nascent stage. The quantum of research has been limited; quality not yet mature enough for assessment; its publication has been scattered and its difficult accessibility has been the nightmare of research workers in this country. All this made many a research workers reinvent the fire and the wheel. At a time when meaningful and relevant research on various aspects of mental retardation is a priority requirement for policy planning one becomes painfully aware that not even reference listing is available for those interested. The pains-taking work undertaken by the authors will go a long way in overcoming this hiatus. Scanning the issues of well over a 100 journals and selecting nearly 1600 papers related to disability is not an easy task. Despite the fact that the authors have avoided doing a qualitative evaluation of the studies because of their commited belief that a time has not yet come to undertake such an exercise, they have given a direction to their work by further indexing and classifying the available papers as also looking into the question as to what are the potentialities of the past work for utilisation in the future.

The present work will for ever be a baseline of what has been carried out in India in the field of mental retardation by way of research in the first fifty years of the active phase of work beginning from the early forties. Simultaneously it will prove to be a spring board for action for research professional workers who decide to work in this area. Some of the findings may prove to be disturbing. For example, when some pioneering efforts were made by committed individuals to start journals and thus encourage research publications in the field of disability in general and mental retardation in particular there was minimal research work worth the name. Unfortunately, when the research work has started gaining momentum three of these journals have been wiped out of existence. The Indian Journal of Mental Retardation-the official organ of the All India Association on Mental Retardation - which started as an exclusive publication in 1968 could not sustain itself even for two decades. All this may be difficult to accept but one has no other option but to face reality and cope. In scanning, listing and analysing the broad trends of research studies done in India in the field of mental retardation the authors have not only gone over the history of research in this field but in so doing have created history themselves. What Rice and Kamat did for assessment; Jai Vakeel for services and Joginder Gandhi for organisational issues the present work of the authors has achieved for the field of research-yet another land mark and a turning point.

Dr. G.G. Prabhu

Professor & Head, Department of Clinical Psychology & Dean, Faculty of Mental Health and Neuro Sciences, National Institute of Mental Health and Neuro Sciences, Bangalore University, Bangalore

PREFACE

Research in the area of disability and impairments, especially mental handicaps, is a bourgeoning phenomenon in post-independent India. There are a handful of scientific journals which carry research publications on mental handicaps regularly. Apart from these, few medical and social science journals also carry one or two articles on mental retardation in between their several issues.

A problem that frequently confronts avid social scientists in the field of mental retardation in India is the accessibility to matching references for their proposed problem area chosen for investigation. One may browse through Psychological Abstracts, MEDLARS, ERIC, Disability Abstracts Database, Mental Health Abstracts, Index Medicus, Excerpta Medicus, etc., to acquire information about few foreign publications in the chosen area of interest. However, there is no exclusive source of reference listing available for research already done within the country. Often, the research scholar has to content with a patchy review of literature drawn from nearby incomplete sources. This depresses the quality of research and leads many investigators into the blind alley of working on the same topics that have been already worked on by others. Such duplication of research work and wastage of research time is ill afforded in a country like India.

The history of research in the field of rehabilitation sciences, especially mental handicaps, can be traced only through the last fifty years in India. After several initial hiccups owing to lack of trained social scientists, constraints on funds and resources, etc., there is some semblance of serious and sustained research work in the field only since the last twenty years. The International Year of Disabled Persons (IYDP) in 1981 appears to have provided the needed impetus to recognising the problems of disabled persons by researchers in rehabilitation sciences.

Indeed, the present time is premature to evaluate the quality of research on disability and impairments in India. However, the time is at least ripe enough to take stock and review the quantum of research work that has gone by in the last few decades. This exercise is to serve as a baseline on available research for later comparison of progression and/or regression over time. Besides, the present stock taking can serve as a lamp post to direct the course of future research in this area. It can reflect issues related to expansion of research into unanswered questions, deceleration of interest on often harped or over studied issues, innovation along new lines, etc., in the field of disability and impairments. Further, there are groups of professional researchers, who evince keen interest to work on transcultural aspects of disability and impairments cutting across national or regional borders. A compilation of existing research on disability and impairments, particularly mental handicaps, is highly warranted in the light of all the above mentioned needs.

In view of these prevailing difficulties for researchers, the authors embarked on a project over the last few years to collect all articles/papers published by Indian authors in Indian journals on any or all aspects of mental retardation. All Indian contributions to foriegn journals and foriegn contributions to Indian Journals in this area were excluded. The long and arduous search yielded a compiled list of over one thousand five hundred articles/research papers published in over 100 Indian journals on various topics in the field of disability and impairments.

The present book is intended to share this compilation with interested professionals, colleagues working with handicapped persons, planners and policy makers, budding research scholars in universities or institutions for handicapped persons, foreign researchers inclined towards studying transcultural aspects of handicapping conditions, etc.

The book carries research titles on all disability and impairments alongwith related titles on areas of general work, including, child development, epilepsies, conduct disorders, mental illnesses, etc. Admittedly, the emphasis of the present search is only on mental retardation. Therefore, the likely chances of finding research titles related to other handicapping conditions is lower when compared to mental retardation *per se*. Even with regard to research titles on mental retardation, no claim is made that it is exhaustive. There is every possibility that some articles could have escaped the searching eyes of the authors. The availability of past journals was a major problem for the present investigators. Despite access to impressive libraries and documentation centres available in the country, such as, National Institute for the Mentally Handicapped, Secunderabad; National Institute of Mental Health and Neuro Sciences, Bangalore; Bangalore University, Bangalore; College of Social Work, Hyderabad; College of Nursing, Hyderabad; Osmania University, Hyderabad; Gandhi Medical College, Hyderabad; Osmania Medical College, Hyderabad; Institute of Mental Health, Hyderabad; etc., there were instances when specific issues of particular journals were unavailable for the present search. Wherein the authors took recourse to using cross references from published articles, there were several instances when the cross citations were either incorrect or incomplete. Particularly, there was a problem in obtaining issue numbers for several articles. This was partially due to the numbering practices followed by different journals. Therefore, one is likely to find issue numbers of some articles missing in the present edition. There were instances when the investigators found the same article published twice in two different journals. This could be due to the publication policy of some journals, which do not insist on contributors providing exclusive publication rights or giving an undertaking that their publications are not simultaneously sent for print elsewhere.

The present book has been divided into nine separate sections covering different types of diagnostic conditions. They are:

I. Mental handicaps
II. Physical handicaps
III. Speech and hearing handicaps
IV. Visual impairment
V. Infantile autism
VI. Cerebral palsy
VII. Juvenile delinquency
VIII. Learning disabilities
IX. General (others)

Every citation in this book is serially numbered and placed within its appropriate section, depending on the target population on which the specific study was undertaken. In rare instances, if an article was worked on comparative conditions (say, hearing handicaps with visual impairments), we have taken the liberty of placing the said article in one section in preference for the other. However, the ideal procedure to locate a specific article or set of references on a topic is to browse through Subject Index. The Subject Index denotes the specific numbers of those articles which is related to it. The Authors Index facilitates approaching the search for a specific title from the names of well known authorities on specific topics in the field of disability and impairments.

A list of addresses of libraries and documentation centres in the field of disability and impairments in the country is also appended at the end of the book. This is to facilitate research scholars approaching the respective centres with request for photocopies of the articles of their requirement or interest. Alternatively, users may appproach the address of the private consultancy, supervised by one of the authors. The Consultancy provides Computerised Bibliography Services (CBS) and posts print outs of research titles or photocopies of available articles on request. The details of these data service is given in appendices.

We welcome additions, alterations, revisions and suggestions from esteemed readers for any further refinement of this book.

S.Venkatesan
V.G.D. Vepuri

ACKNOWLEDGMENTS

No product of human industry can be truly claimed as the sole propriety of one or two individuals alone. Inevitably, every work is the result of a complex confluence between several recognised or unrecognised variables. This is particularly true for the origin and completion of this compilation work.

What started as a transient and desultory interest to browse for past research titles on mental handicaps in India, soon acquired the proportion of an outrageous obsession for us to scan every page in all sorts of available journals. Many times, our search went on ravenously unmindful of the unearthly hours that we were trespassing. We are extremely gratuitous to our forbearing family members, expecially our parents, wives (Shoba and Bhavani) and our kids (Viba and Sruti). They have all been accommodating to the vagaries of our working schedules and even spared us from our domestic roles and responsibilities during the course of this ardous pursuit to complete this book.

We are also thankful to the officers-in-charge of the libraries that we have visited during the course of this compilation. They were kind enough to grant us permission to use their centres and also helped us in locating specific issues of misplaced journals.

We are thankful to our employers, Dr. D.K. Menon, Director, National Institute for the Mentally Handicapped, Secunderabad and Dr. P.Hanumantha Rao, Chairman, Sweekaar, Rehabilitation Institute for Handicapped, Secunderabad, who have been a constant source of encouragement in all our academic pursuits in the feild of disability and impairments.

We reserve a special word of thanks to Dr G G Prabhu, Professor and Head, Department of Clinical Psychology, National Institute of Mental Health and Neuro Sciences, Bangalore, for having favourably responded, at our request, to foreword this book and guiding us in collecting certain research titles. We deem it a great honour bestowed upon us by a pioneer advocate for sceintific research in the field of mental handicaps in India.

Admittedly, it is impossible to list everyone who has directly or indirectly contributed to the making of this book. We will be failing in our duty if we do not place on record the services rendered by Mr. C.Ravi, Computer Programmer, who has regularly lent his help in documenting this work.

We leave it that every trifle nod of appreciation received from any quarter has elevated our zeal to work towards the completion of this book.

S. Venkatesan
V.G.D. Vepuri

CONTENTS

MENTAL RETARDATION IN INDIA:
An Overview

Introduction

India is a vast country covering over 3.3 million square kilometres and occupying a strategic geographical location in southern Asia. In terms of population, India is the second largest country after China. It contains 16 per cent of the world's population and has only 2.2 per cent of its area. As per 1991 census, India's population is estimated at 843.93 million, spread unevenly across 25 States and 7 Union Territories. More than 75 per cent of the population live in rural areas, while about 10 per cent of them are increasingly becoming part of a newly evolving marginal habitat - semi urban areas. The remaining population dwell in urban areas.

Prevalence of Mental Retardation

India has not conducted any national survey on the nature and magnitude of disability and impairments in the country. The Census Organisation used to collect data on physical infirmities in the decennial census during 1861 to 1941. This practice was discontinued owing to doubts regarding the reliability of such data. This practice was partially resumed in 1981. However, no information was gathered regarding prevalence of persons with mental handicaps. In the past, some sample surveys have attempted to estimate the prevalence of mentally handicapped population in select areas. But, a total picture does not emerge from these surveys. Even the National Sample Survey on Disabled Persons carried out in 1981 has sadly excluded mental disability from its purview. Any proposal for conduct of a National Survey of mental disabilities is beset with problems related to financial outlay, difficult terrain to traverse along the length and breadth of the country, multi-lingualism, paucity of trained manpower to undertake such exercises, etc.

A few sample surveys have used psychometric tests and labelled approximately three per cent of the general population as "mentally retarded". This implies that the retarded population in India could be anywhere near the alarming figure of 26 million.

Role of Government

In pre-independent India, there was practically no initiative from the government to introduce any services for persons with mental handicaps. Neither, there was any demand to initiate services for these persons since public awareness on mental disabilities was dismally low. Besides, public attitudes towards mentally disabled persons oscillated ambivalently between pity, tolerance or superstition at one end to apathy or ignorance at the other.

It was against this background that in 1950, for the first time, Government of India recognised disabled persons as an equal and rightful participants in the social and economic activities of the nation. This was guaranteed by the Constitution of India before Central and State Governments began expressing concern for welfare of the disabled by initiating several programmes or schemes for these persons.

a) *Welfare Sector*

As recently as on 25th September, 1985, the Central Government constituted a new Ministry of Welfare by bringing the subject of handicapped welfare under one of its five bureaus. In contemporary India, the responsibility of implementing welfare schemes for the handicapped is shared between Central as well as State governments. Broadly, the Centre is responsible for formulating welfare polices and programmes apart from coordinating, guiding or promoting implementation of welfare services by State governments.

In order to effectively deal with the multi-dimensional problems of the handicapped, the Central government established four national institutes, one in each area of disability.

The National Institute for the Mentally Handicapped (NIMH), Secunderabad, was established in 1984 as an autonomous body under Ministry of Welfare, Government of India. The NIMH is to serve as an apex organisation for manpower development, growth of suitable models of service delivery and for undertaking research in areas related to early identification, training and rehabilitation of persons with mental handicaps. The NIMH is also to serve as a premier information and documentation centre in the area of metal retardation.

Apart form the recently established NIMH, there are other national bodies in the country which are also actively engaged in research, training and service programmes for the mentally handicapped. Some of them are:

i) All India Institute of Physical Medicine and Rehabilitation,

Bombay;

ii) All India Institute of Speech and Hearing, Mysore;

iii) Government Institute of Rehabilitation and Artificial Limbs, Madras;

iv) The Institute for Physically Handicapped, New Delhi;

v) The National Institute of Rehabilitation Training and Research, Orissa;

vi) All India Institute of Medical Sciences, New Delhi;

vii) National Institute of Mental Health and Neurosciences, Bangalore.

The Ministry of Welfare has also set up a National Council on Handicapped Welfare to frame policy guidelines for the entire country and to determine priorities. The Government of India has special schemes for granting annual National Awards for outstanding employers of persons with mental handicap as well as employees with mental disabilities. This serves as an incentive for people to come forward and employ mentally retarded persons. Other beneficial schemes for the mentally handicapped are travel concessions in Indian Railways, Children's Educational Allowance, providing reimbursement of Rs. 50 per month to Central Government employees having children with mental handicaps. Besides, there are income-tax concessions for parents of the mentally handicapped children. Recently a comprehensive scheme for providing Community Based Rehabilitation Services (CBRS) for mentally handicapped persons hailing from rural areas has also been initiated by the Ministry.

b) ***Education Sector***

Some of the policies and programmes adopted by Ministry of Education, Government of India, has fringe benefits for children with mental handicap. Article 45 of the Indian Constitution emphasises that the State shall provide free and compulsory education for all children up to the age of 14. Based on the recommendations of several educational commissions set up by the Central Government form time to time, a National Education Policy (NEP) was enunciated in 1968. This policy provides the framework for educational expansion and development in the country. The salient features of NEP, which has relevance for mentally handicapped children, is its emphsises on provision for free and compulsory educational facilities, encouragement of Integrated Education Programmes (IEP), provision for basic resource facilities in selected educational institutions, promotion of integration of mentally handicapped children with normal or non-disabled children, etc.

The Ministry of Welfare introduced a scheme for Integrated Education for Disabled (IED) Children on an experimental basis in few states in 1974. Most of the benefits of this on going Scheme appears to reach only children with physical and/or sensory disabilities rather than the mentally handicapped children.

c) *Labour Sector*

The Ministry of Labour, Government of India has been providing another source of succour for the disabled population in the country through some of its policies and programmes. The right to work and the right to public assistance in case of unemployment, provision for just and humane working conditions, minimum wages and ensuing decent standards of living are all severally recognised in different articles of the Constitution of India.

The overall employment scene for able bodied persons is itself at nascent stage in the country. Therefore, any discussion on creating employment opportunities for disabled persons, especially mentally disabled, is likely to pose radical questions on the very feasibility of such endeavours. However, there can be no two opinions on the need for providing work to the disabled citizens of the country especially in the view of adverse effects on the economy, wherein a tenth of the disabled population is workless and consequently their burden is to be shared by the non-disabled sections of society.

Some of the important programmes to promote employment for the disabled in the country include, reservation of jobs in public sector, creation of special employment exchanges for handicapped, establishment of vocational rehabilitation centers to train or place disabled persons, grant-in-aid assistance to voluntary organisations for training and employment for disabled persons, etc. However, most of these programmes do not seem to directly benefit individuals with mental handicap as much as those with other physical and/or sensory disabilities. For example, employment exchange data reveals that about 40,000 handicapped persons have registered themselves annually over the last four years. About 90 per cent of the registrants are physically disabled, six per cent are blind and the remaining are speech and hearing impaired. There is hardly any scope for registration of mentally handicapped individuals.

Role of Voluntary Organisations

In India the voluntary sector continues to play a dominant and significant role in providing welfare and rehabilitation services for the disabled. A large number of voluntary agencies have emerged in several parts of the country in aid of the handicapped. Before Independence, many of these voluntary organisations thrived on small contributions from philanthropists or well wishers. This trend has changed recently as these organisations are increasingly becoming dependent upon grants from government and industrial establishments. Tax concessions granted by government to the individuals and industrial houses for their contribution towards welfare of handicapped has encouraged flow of funds into voluntary sector. Besides, some private foreign funding agencies have also been providing financial and material supports to voluntary organisations working for welfare of the handicapped.

Many voluntary agencies not only provide services, but also, act as potential pressure groups. While some voluntary organistions have the means to enlist professional assistance for carrying out their service activities, many of them suffer from problems owing to lack of funds, poor man-management technologies, absence of incisive professionalism, etc.

There are broadly two types of voluntary organisations serving the mentally handicapped in the country. They are:

i) Those organised on humanitarian conditions by well meaning philanthropists or social activists; and,
ii) Those which owe their origin to the parents or relatives of the mentally handicapped persons.

The motivation behind voluntarism in the area of mental handicap has also undergone considerable metamorphosis over the years in India. Most voluntary agencies started in the early independence days were raised on religious zeal and frank sentimentalism in favour of doing "good" to the "unfortunately" disabled as an "act of service to god". Even today, few voluntary agencies serve the mentally handicapped on such premises and are manned/supervised by missionaries of different religious faiths or by retired senior citizens with a fervour to spend the last days of their life for a "noble cause". Even if the emotional foundations of such voluntary agencies are commendable and qualify them to initiate services for mentally handicapped persons, to sustain quality services may require sound scientific persistance for marketing a "cause", which is lacking.

Some voluntary agencies have been initiated by parents or relatives of mentally handicapped persons. At times, parents self help voluntarism has evolved as a result of their felt dissatisfaction or distrust about philanthropist activities.

The contemporary emphasis is on building awareness amongst parents of mentally handicapped so as to enable them to form their own self help groups. Parents are encouraged to register their associations or self help groups and even enlist professional support to run the service centre for their own children with mental handicaps. The initial experiments along these lines are proving to be, both, popular as well as successful with many parent organisations. Some parent self help groups have even gone to the extent of availing Group Insurance Schemes to ensure adequate economic and social security benefits for their children with mental handicaps. As on date, there are about forty parent self help groups scattered across the country.

Voluntarism in mental retardation is yet to come of age and maturity in India. The professional interactions between voluntary agencies are far from being mutually cooperative or coordinated. Each agency works in isolation so as to aggrandise their own self image than in the common endeavour to promote the cause of handicap welfare. This has led to some degree of slowness in the pace of welfare for individuals with mental handicap.

Growth of Institutions

The Home for Mentally Deficient Children, Bombay, established by Children's Aid Society, in 1941, is claimed to be the first voluntary agency in India. In the fifties, eleven more schools were started in various parts of the country. Another sixty centres were added during the sixties.

The NIMH has compiled a Directory of Institutions for Mentally Handicapped Persons in India (Reddy, 1988; 1989; 1992) in order to derive a comprehensive picture on the nature and distribution of available services in the country. By the year ending 1992, the Directory (and its supplements) have listed 485 institutions serving mentally handicapped persons spread over 19 states and 4 union territories. There are, still, six States and three Union Territories, which are not represented. The situation is particularly grim in the North-Eastern States, wherein services for mentally retarded persons are conspicuous by their absence.

Even wherein services are available, their pattern of distribution is far from being equitable or commensurate with the population/prevalence demands in that area. Fortunately, Government of India has recognised this unevenness in distribution of available services and is currently encouraging stimulation of services in unrepresented areas. There has been a three fold increase in the number of institutions for persons with mental handicaps compared to a baseline figure of around 150 agencies in 1980's. However, one must be cautious of the fact that a small percentage of these institutions listed on record may not even exist on ground, or maybe, planning to start services in due course of time.

The mere availability of institutional facilities for mentally handicapped persons cannot be considered as adequate unless the quality of such rendered services are also elaborated. Unfortunately, there is a lot to be desired from the quality of services rendered by some voluntary organisations.

Professionalism

Advances in the field of modern medicine has succeeded in improving the average life span of, both, mentally disabled as well as the non-disabled population. The decrease in infant mortality rates owing to increased awareness about pre-natal, natal and post-natal care, immunisation practices, prevention programmes, etc., has also contributed to a possible increase in incidence of the severe-profound categories of mental handicaps (cases that would have otherwise seen their natural demise).

Individuals with mental handicap require scientifically planned and well integrated services from the professionals, such as, peadiatrician, clinical psychologist, psychiatrist, special teacher, occupational therapist, speech therapist, physiotherapist, etc.

Before 1985, there were only about ten centers offering some form of Certificate/Diploma level courses for special teachers of children with mental handicaps. At present, there are over twenty centers which offer diploma level training to in service candidates/teachers from voluntary organisations. A uniform syllabi is prescribed for the teacher trainees, who take a common annual examination conducted by the NIMH, Secunderabad. The NIMH also offers a Bachelors Degree in Mental Retardation affiliated to Osmania University, Hyderabad. The objective of this course is to train a student to provide comprehensive service for mentally handicapped persons.

A recently compiled "Directory of Professionals in Mental Handicap in India" (Reddy, 1991) lists 795 professionals from 19 states in the country. Only 28 (3.52 %) of them are trained till doctorate level, 25 (3.15%) are at pre-doctoral level, 156 (19.63 %) are at Master's level and 87 (10.94 %) are with graduate qualifications. Out of the remaining, 223 (28.05 %) are graduates with professional diplomas or certificates in mental retardation and 139 (17.48 %) are undergraduates with professional diplomas or certificates in mental retardation. Besides, there are also 137 (17.23 %) untrained persons listed in the Directory.

Admittedly, the names listed in the Directory cannot be, by any means, exhaustive. Nor do they reflect the actual state of affairs regarding manpower resources in mental retardation in India. There are several reasons for this suspicion. The mobility of persons working in the area of mental handicaps in India is very high. Many unemployed persons may work temporarily in the field until they secure better job opportunities elsewhere. The teacher income in an average special school setting is very low. Despite government recommendations on salaries for special teachers; in actual job situations, one has to brave the option of a lesser pay then the dangerous reality of remaining unemployed.

Research

The advancements in any field is often the direct result of increasing experiences as well as controlled scientific research. In the field of mental retardation, scientific research has always had a low priority. A peep into the history of mental retardation in India shows concerted efforts only by a handful of investigators. Often, owing to their individual competencies such individuals have succeeded in completing certain projects on particular aspects of mental retardation. Otherwise, research literature is replete with elaborations on specific medical syndromes, anecdotal reports, case histories or even frank sentimental advocacy in favour of the 'cause' of mental retardation. These observations do not amount to carping at the contributions already made in this relatively neglected field. Rather, it is the expression of an earnest desire to concert and coordinate a research policy or programmes for better understanding of a vexing reality: Mental Retardation.

REFERENCES

Ramaswamy, U. 1990: *Non Government Organisation in India.* New Delhi: Ebert Foundation.

Reddy, S.H.K. 1988: *Directory of institutions for mentally handicapped persons in India.* Secunderabad: NIMH.

Reddy, S.H.K. 1989: *Directory of institutions for mentally handicapped persons in India* Secunderabad: NIMH.

Reddy, S.H.K. 1991: *Directory of professionals in India.* Secunderabad: NIMH.

Reddy, S.H.K. 1992: *Directory of institutions for mentally handicapped persons in India.* Secunderabad: NIMH.

RESEARCH ON MENTAL RETARDATION IN INDIA: A Qualitative and Quantitative Analysis

Introduction

Objective observation, experimentation, systematic law making and derivation of inferences on experienced phenomena is the main endeavour in any branch of Science. The acquired scientific knowledge is publicly disseminated by means of presentation in seminars, conferences, publication of books, journals, etc. Scientific research in the field of disability and impairments, especially mental retardation, is still at a nascent stage in India.

The first Indian journal in the field of mental retardation was the *Occupational Therapy Journal* later renamed as *The Journal of Rehabilitation in Asia* appeared from Bombay in 1960. With the formation of All India Association on Mental Retardation (AIAMR), Chandigarh, *The Indian Journal of Mental Retardation* appeared in 1968. Thereafter, the Federation for Welfare of the Mentally Retarded (FWMR), New Delhi, started a popular journal titled *Mental Retardation Digest* in 1970. None of these pioneering journals appear any more in the country. In fact, in the contemporary scene, there is no single journal exclusively publishing research articles on mental handicaps only. Rather, there are a few journals with generic interest on all disabilities and impairments. For example, *Disabilities and Impairments* is an interdisciplinary biannual research journal on all handicaps published from New Delhi since 1985. The Ministry of Welfare, Government of India, brings out *The Indian Journal of Disability and Rehabilitation* twice in a year since 1987. Mostly, research articles on mental retardation are currently published in discipline oriented journals, such as, *Indian Pediatrics, Indian Journal of Clinical Psychology, Indian Journal of Social Work,* etc.

Research in the field of rehabilitation sciences appear to be advancing at a rapid pace in the West as well as India. This is evidenced by the increasing number of research publications on topics related to disability and impairments. Despite these gradual developments, there has been no attempt to undertake a kind of stock taking on the quality and quantity of publications in the field of mental retardation in India.

It was the aim of the present study to compile a list of research titles for articles published on mental retardation in India; and, to study broad trends in the distribution of publications in relation to specific variables, such as, years, type of journal, areas of research, etc.

Methodology

The investigators approached every known/available information and documentation centre on social sciences (Appendix 1) for procuring old issues of journals. Each journal/issue was searched for research articles published on any area related to disability and impairments, especially mental retardation.

The following inclusion/exclusion criteria were maintained during the literature search:

Inclusion Criteriao

Any or all research titles related to the field of mental retardation published by Indian authors in Indian journals were included. Research articles bordering on indirect references to any aspect of mental retardation (such as, general morbidity studies on mental health conditions) were also included.

Exclusion Criteria

Any or all research articles not related directly to the field of mental retardation, or were related to the field of mental retardation but published by foreign authors in Indian journals or by Indian authors in foreign journals were excluded. References quoting mimeographs, books, proceedings of conferences or seminars, video films, etc., were also excluded from the purview of the present search. As far as possible, cross references were avoided in view of the fact that they were at times incomplete, incorrect or even misleading.

The compiled list of references were periodically fed into a computer on specially designed bibliography software programme.

Results

The literature search yielded an overall 1589 research titles related to different fields of disability and impairments from 102 Indian Journals. The details of top fifteen journals in this bibliography on mental retardation, such as, it periodicity, year of first publication, the years and number of issues screened are given in Table 1.

Table 1: Distribution of Top Fifteen Journal Research for the Present Bibliography

Rank order	Name of Journal	Year of first publication	Periodicity	Screened	
				Years	Issues
I	*Indian Journal of Pediatrics*	1933	Bimonthly	52-93	258
II	*Indian Pediatrics*	1964	Monthly	64-93	360
III	*Indian Journal of Mental Retardation**	1968	Halfyearly	68-82	30
IV	*Indian Journal of Medical Research*	1912	Monthly	54-93	480
V	*The Journal of Rehabilitation in Asia**	1960	Quarterly	60-87	112
VI	*Child Psychiatry Quarterly**	1968	Quarterly	68-89	88
VII	*Indian Journal of Psychiatry*	1959	Half yearly	65-92	56
VIII	*Indian Journal of Disability & Rehabilitation*	1987	Half yearly	87-92	12
IX	*The Indian Journal of Social Work*	1940	Quarterly	40-92	212
X	*Indian Journal of Clinical Psychology*	1974	Half yearly	74-92	38
XI	*Indian Journal of Child Health**	1952	Monthly	52-63	144
XII	*Social Welfare*	1952	Monthly	57-87	372
XIII	*Disabilities & Impairments*	1987	Half yearly	87-92	12
XIV	*Journal of Personality & Clinical Studies**	1985	Half yearly	85-92	16
XV	*The Nursing Journal of India*	1920	Monthly	64-92	348
	Mental Health Review	1981	Half yearly	81-91	22

*indicates Journals that have ceased publication currently.

These top fifteen journals, between themselves, cover 913 out of 1095 (83.4%) research articles on mental retardation in this bibliography (Table 2). In other words, only 182 articles (16.62%) are shared by the remaining 87 journals screened for this bibliography.

In the present bibliography, 1095 (68.91%) reserch titles are directly related to the field of mental retardation (Table 3). The other fields covered under this bibliography are physical handicaps (N: 113; 7.11%), juvenile delinquency (N: 90; 5.66%), speech and hearing handicaps (N: 79; 4.97%), visual impairments (N:26; 1.63%), infantile

Table 2 : Journal-wise Distribution of Research Titles within the Area of Mental Retardation

Rank order	Name of Journal	N	Per cent	Cumulative
I	*Indian Journal of Pediatrics*	215	19.63	19.63
II	*Indian Pediatrics*	133	12.15	31.78
III	*Indian Journal of Mental Retardation*	132	12.06	43.84
IV	*Indian Journal of Medical Research*	69	6.30	50.14
V	*The Journal of Rehabilitation in Asia*	51	4.66	54.80
VI	*Child Psychiatry Quarterly*	45	4.11	58.91
VII	*Indian Journal of Psychiatry*	42	3.84	62.75
VIII	*Indian Journal of Disability & Rehabilitation*	37	3.38	66.13
IX	*The Indian Journal of Social Work*	36	3.29	69.42
X	*Indian Journal of Clinical Psychology*	34	3.11	72.53
XI	*Indian Journal of Child Health*	32	2.92	75.45
XII	*Social Welfare*	25	2.28	77.73
XIII	*Disabilities & Impairments*	22	2.01	79.74
XIV	*Journal of Personality & Clinical Studies*	16	1.46	81.20
XV	*The Nursing Journal of India*	12	1.10	82.30
	Mental Health Review	12	1.10	83.40
	Others	182	16.62	100.00
	Total	**1095**		

Table 3 : Field Wise Distribution of Research Titles

Area	N	Per cent
Mental retardation	1095	68.91
Physical handicaps	113	7.11
Juvenile delinquency	90	5.66
Speech and hearing handicaps	79	4.97
Visual impairment	39	2.45
Cerebral palsy	26	1.63
Infantile autism	15	0.94
Learning disability	4	0.24
Others	128	7.96
Total	**1589**	

Table 4 : Glossary for Topic-wise Distribution of Research Titles on Mental Retardation

1. Medical:

covers specific diagnostic categories/conditions, syndromes (except Downs syndrome), aetiological factors like biochemical, neurological, nutritional, genetic, etc.

2. Psychological:

covers assessment, diagnostic testing, experimental studies on various cognitive aspects, application of behaviour modification techniques, counselling, etc.

3. Psychoeducational:

covers intervention, training, treatment or programme planning and evaluation of teaching strategies; leisure, sport, or curriculum aspects, etc.

4. Policy issues:

covers topics of general disucussion on or about broad policy issues, national planning, etc.

5. Psychosocial:

covers topics related to parental/societal perceptions, family experiences, social or public attitudes, social securities, etc.

6. Downs syndrome:

covers any or all aspects of persons with Downs anamoly

7. Early intervention services:

covers any or all aspects of early detection, screening, and intervention for children at risk as well as those with identified developmental delays

Table 5 : Aspect-wise Distribution of Research Titles within the Area of Mental Retardation

Aspects	N	Per cent
Medical	439	40.09
Psychological	194	17.72
Psychosocial	122	11.14
Policy issues	102	9.32
Psychoeducational	94	8.58
Downs syndrome	55	5.02
Prevalence	38	3.47
Services	26	2.37
Early intervention services	25	2.28
Total	**1095**	

autism (N: 15; 0.95%), learning disabilities (N: 4; 0.24 %) and others (N: 128; 7.95%) respectively. The 'others' category includes research titles of general interest, such as, conduct disorders, seizure disorders, behaviour problems in children, etc.

Admittedly, the emphasis of present bibliography search has confined to the field of mental retardation. Based on a glossary prepared for this purpose (Table 4), an area-wise distributional analysis of the bibliography on mental retardation was carried out on seven distinctly identified areas, viz., medical, psychological, psychoeducational, policy issues, psychosocial, Downs syndrome and early intervention services.

The results of area wise distributional analysis based on the above mentioned glossary, reveals that most research on mental retardation has concentrated on medical aspects (N: 439; 40.09%), followed by focus on psychological aspects (N: 194; 17.72%). psychosocial aspects (N: 122; 11.14%), policy issues (N: 102; 9.32%), psychoeducational aspects (N: 94; 8.58%), Downs syndrome (N: 55; 5.02%), prevalence or epidemiological aspects (N: 38; 3.47%), services deliver (N: 26; 2.37%) and early intervention services (N: 25; 2.28%) respectively (Table 5).

Further, intense analysis was carried out to discover the distribution of research titles in the bibliography in relation to specific topics within the broad areas of medical, psychological, psychoeducational and psychosocial aspects of mental retardation (Table 6).

The results indicate that mental retardation research has covered mainly topics like biochemical anamolies (N: 75; 17.08%), followed

Table 6: Distribution of Research Titles within Specific Topics in the Field of Mental Retardation

Area	N	Percentage
Medical		
Biochemical anamolies	75	17.08
Nutritional disorders	69	15.49
Natal aspects	42	9.57
Meningitis	35	7.97
Congenital malformations	36	8.20
Genetic disorders	30	6.83
Prenatal aspects	19	4.33
Postnatal aspects	19	4.33
Neurological aspects	12	2.73
Tuberous sclerosis	12	2.73
Muscular dystrophies	11	2.51
Trichobezoars	11	2.51
Consanguinity	10	2.43
Encephalopathies	9	2.28
Hormonal disturbances	8	1.82
Psychological		
Diagnostic assessment	53	27.32
Nature of MR	28	14.43
Behaviour Modification	21	10.82
Cognitive researches	20	10.31
Counselling & psychotherapy	16	8.25
Developmental aspects	9	4.64
Speech and language aspects	8	4.12
Psychoeducational		
Teaching/Training aspects	47	38.52
Play/Leisure/Recreation	16	13.11
Vocational aspects	14	11.48
Psychosocial		
Attitude's and others' perceptions	33	35.12
Parental aspects	13	13.83
Adjustment/adaptations	10	10.64
OTHERS	409	
Total	439	

Table 7: Year Wise Distribution of Research Titles within the Field of Mental Retardation

Duration (in years)	N	Per cent	Cumulative Per cent
< 1960	77	7.03	7.03
1961 - 1965	86	7.85	14.88
1966 - 1970	185	16.90	31.78
1971 - 1975	179	16.35	48.13
1976 - 1980	165	15.07	63.20
1981 - 1985	172	15.71	78.91
1986 - 1990	184	16.80	95.71
1991 +	47	4.29	100.00
Total	**1095**		

(Range: 1936-1993; 58 years; Mean: 18.44)

by investigations on nutritional disorders (N: 69; 15.49%) and so on. A bulk of psychological research on mental retardation has been devoted towards disagnostic assessment (N: 53; 27.32%), followed by writings on nature of mental retardation (N: 28; 14.43%) and so on. Psychoeducational research on mental retardation has studied teaching or training aspects (N: 47; 38.52%), followed by topics related to play/leisure/recreational aspects (N: 16; 13.11%) and vocational aspects (N: 14; 11.48%). Psychosocial research on mental retardation has frequently studied attitudes and others' perception (N: 33; 35.12%) followed by parent studies (N: 13; 13.83%) and articles on adjustment/adaptation problems in this population (N: 10; 10.64%).

A year wise distribution of research titles within the field of mental retardation (Table 7) shows an initial spurt in the quantity of research after the year 1965 compared to the period before. However, there appears to be a more or less stable production of research papers in the past 25 years.

Discussion

The present bibliography is a compilation of 1095 (68.99%) research titles directly related to the field of mental retardation from an overall 1587 listings in the field of disability and impairments (Table Three). A cursory analysis shows that *Indian Journal of Pediatrics* ranks first with the highest number of research publications on mental retardation

Table 8 : Average Number of Publications per issue on Mental Retardation in the Top fifteen Journals

Rank order	Name of Journal	N	Number of Issues Screened	Mean articles per issue
I	*Indian Journal of Pediatrics*	215	258	0.833
II	*Indian Pediatrics*	133	360	0.369
III	*Indian Journal of Mental Retardation*	132	30	4.400
IV	*Indian Journal of Medical Research*	69	480	0.143
V	*The Journal of Rehabilitation in Asia*	51	112	0.455
VI	*Child Psychiatry Quarterly*	45	88	0.511
VII	*Indian Journal of Psychiatry*	42	56	0.750
VIII	*Indian Journal of Disability & Rehabilitation*	37	12	3.083
IX	*The Indian Journal of Social Work*	36	212	0.169
X	*Indian Journal of Clinical Psychology*	34	38	0.894
XI	*Indian Journal of Child Health*	32	144	0.222
XII	*Social Welfare*	25	372	0.005
XIII	*Disabilities & Impairments*	22	12	1.833
XIV	*Journal of Personality & Clinical Studies*	16	16	1.000
XV	*The Nursing Journal of India*	12	348	0.034
	Mental Health Review	12	22	0.545
	Others	182		
	Total	1095		

(N: 215; 19.63%) followed by *Indian Pediatrics* (N: 133; 12.15%). *Indian Journal of Mental Retardation* (N: 132; 12.06%) and so on (Table 2.2). However, this picture is quite different when the mean number of publications per issue in the top fifteen ranked journals are computed (Table 8).

Owing to the long standing years of their existence and/ or due to greater frequency in their periodicity of publication (Table 1), it appears

Table 9 : Decade-wise Distribution of Research in Different Areas

Areas	Years					Total
	< 1960	1961-70	1971-80	1981-90	1990+	
Medical	57	152	142	79	9	439
Psychological	7	39	81	58	9	250
Psychosocial	1	12	36	64	9	122
Policy	6	13	34	46	3	102
Psychoeducational	3	11	29	45	6	94
Downs syndrome	1	11	13	27	3	55
Prevalence	1	7	16	13	1	38
Services	1	5	6	8	6	26
Early Intervention Services	-	-	7	15	3	25
Total	77	250	364	355	49	1095

that *Indian Journal of Pediatrics* and *Indian Pediatrics* have gained the top slots for their higher number of articles on mental handicaps. On the contrary, when the frequency of articles on mental retardation per issue is calculated (Table 8), *Indian Journal of Mental Retardation* (N: 132; Mean: 4.4) ranks first followed by *Indian Journal of Disability and Rehabilitation* (N: 37; Mean: 3.083), *Disabilities and Impairments* (N: 16; Mean: 1.833) and so on. Further, it is to be noted that nearly 102 journals are represented in this bibliography and there are hardly any articles on mental retardation appearing in most of them. Probably there is only a token representation of one odd article in between several issues of these many journals. In the contemporary scenario, there is an urgent need to start a Journal exclusively for publications in the field of mental retardation. This need is justified because as many as five out of these top fifteen journals have ceased publishing currently.

The year-wise distribution of research titles within the field of mental retardation (Table 7) reveals an average of about 18.44 publications per year from 1936 to date. This average has almost doubled for the last decade, i.e., between 1981-85 (N: 172; Mean: 34.4) and 1986-90 (N: 184; Mean: 36.8). This implies that about thirty to forty research articles are currently being published on mental retardation every year in India.

As mentioned earlier, the focus of research on mental retardation in India has all along been dominated by medical models. Nearly 439 articles (40.09%) from the present compilation of 1095 titles are on medical aspects of mental retardation. Apart from the several biochemical studies and nutritional studies by noteworthy project teams, others have mainly highlighted specific syndromes, annnotated case reports or correlated specific medical aspects to mental retardation, etc. More significantly, research on preventive aspects and early intervention services have taken a backseat in the scenario of medical research on mental retardation in India. As regards to psychological aspects of mental retardation, research contributions have largely confined themselves to problems of diagnostic assessment (N:53; 27.32%).and on definition of mental handicaps (N: 28; 14.43%) (Table 2.6). These trends in the focus of psychological research appear to be in consonance with the contemporary historical phase through which the field of mental retardation appears to be moving in India. The current phase of diagnostic assessment and identification of persons with mental retardation may soon pave way to more studies related to training/teaching and programme planning for individuals with mental disabilities in the oncoming decades.

Another area of considerable neglect are studies on parents/families of persons with mental handicaps. Wherein the long term objective is to use parent or family resources for the welfare and rehabilitation of mentally handicapped persons, there is likely to be a gradual shift of research interests to these areas in the oncoming years.

These trends and futuristic projections appear justified especially wherein one attempts to study the decade wise shift of priorities on research in mental retardation (Table 9).

It appears that interest on medical aspects of mental retardation research was at its peak during the decades of 1960s and 1970s, with a gradual waning of such interests in the decade of 1980's. On the other hand, research on rehabilitative aspects seem to be on its ascendance in the recent times compared to hardly any such writings in the decades preceeding 1970's (Table 9). It is heartening to note that increased importance is being given to topics like early intervention services, policy issues, psychoeducational training, etc.

Implication of Present Study

1. The present work highlights that mental retardation research in India is proceeding along a determined sequence of interests and historical necessaties. In earlier stages, study of medical aspects of mental retardation was the major preoccupation of

investigators as compared to the current scenario, wherein rehabilitative research is gaining ground in the country.

2. There is need to coordinate and harness the multifarious directions that contemporary research on mental retardation appears to be assuming in India. Otherwise, there is a likely peril of wastage and dissipation of the meagre and precious research resources in the form of repetitive studies under the euphemism of research replication.
3. The results of the study are even suggestive of a need to start a research advisory body exclusive to the field of mental retardation so that there is a pointed direction for researchers to minimise wastage of resources or time.
4. The present bibliography highlights that early intervention, prevention, family studies, integrated education and allied issues continue to ramain as woefully neglected topics of research on mental retardation in contemporary India.

BIBLIOGRAOHY OF QUANTITATIVE ANALYSIS

Mental Retardation

1. Abraham, A., 1990, Behaviour modification in institutionalised mentally retarded children: Case reports. *Journal of Personality and Clinical Studies,* 6 (1): 124-126.
2. Abraham, A., Mishra, H., and Kumaraih, V., 1989, Effectiveness of behaviour modification in institution based mentally retarded children. *Journal of Personality and Clinical Studies,* 5 (3): 153-160
3. Abraham, J., ChakRaoani, B., Singh, M., Kokrady, S., and Bachhawat, B.K., 1969, Hurler's disease: A clinical and biochemical study of a case. *Indian Journal of Medical Research,* 57 (9): 1761-1766.
4. Achar, S.T., and Benjamin, V., 1953, Observations on nutritional dystrophy: Clinical, pathological and biochemical aspects. *Indian Journal of Child Health,* 2 (1): 1.
5. Achar, S.T., and Thambiah, S., 1954, Pyogenic meningitis in children. *Indian Journal of Child Health,* 3 (1): 5.
6. Adiseshiah, W.T.V., 1972, Rehabilitation programme for handicapped people in Madras. *The Indian Journal of Social Work,* 33 (3): 257-268.
7. Agarwal, K.G., 1977 Mental deficiency research in India. *Indian Journal of Mental Retardation,* 10 (2): 70-87.
8. Agarwal, K.G., and Dhar, V., 1983, Causal attribution and disability. *Journal of Psychological Researches,* 32 (2): 81-86.
9. Agarwal, V.K., and Kumar, P., 1969, A follow up study of treated cases of tuberculous meningitis. *Indian Pediatrics,* 6 p 291.
10. Aggarwal, V.P., and Bharadwaj, T.P., 1973, Changes in heptatic ribonucleoproteins in kwashiorkor. *Indian Journal of Pediatrics,* 40 (300): 40.
11. Agrawal, K.G., and Gandhi, J.S. ,1968, A comparative study of

gRaohic and verbal scales in the measurement of affective meaning. *Indian Journal of Mental Retardation,* 1 (2): 75-79.

12. Agrawal, K.G., and Mehta, P., 1976, Work education for the retarded. *Indian Journal of Mental Retardation,* 9 : 45.
13. Agrawal, S.P., Dikshit, S.K., and Tandon, L., 1970, Syndrome of retarded growth, obesity, muscular hypotonia and mental retardation,Prader Willi syndrome, *Indian Journal of Pediatrics,* 37 (266): 105-107.
14. Ahuja, Y.R., 1971, Genetic and cytogenetic aspect of mental retardation. *Child Psychiatry Quarterly,* 4 (1): 6-11.
15. Akhtar, S., and Varma, V.K., 1972, Guidelines for the parents of mentally retarded children. *Indian Journal of Mental Retardation,* 5 (1&2): 75-88.
16. Ambani, L.M., Patel, Z.M., and Dhareshwar, S.S., 1984, Clinical, biochemical and cytogenetic studies in mental retardation. *Indian Journal of Medical Research,* 79 (3): 384-391.
17. Amesur, C.A., 1955, National Advisory Council,NAC, for the education of the handicapped in India. *Indian Journal of Otolaryngology,* 7 (4): 136-143.
18. Amesur, C.A., 1959, Resettlement of the handicapped in India. *Social Welfare,* 6 (6): 21-24.
19. Amesur, C.A., 1959, National Advisory Council,NAC, for the education of the handicapped in India: Second. *Antiseptic,* 46 (9): 713-717.
20. Amesur, C.A., 1960, Nature and extent of the problem of the handicapped. *Social Work Review,* 7 : 313.
21. Amesur, C.A., 1962, Education and rehabilitation of the mentally retarded in India. *The Indian Journal of Social Work,* 23 (2): 167-172.
22. Amla, I., and Narayan, J.V., 1968, Finger nail clubbing in kwashiorkor. *Indian Journal of Pediatrics,* 35 (240): 19-22.
23. Amla, I., and Punekar, B.D., 1968, The results of routine screening for phenylketonuria and galactosemia in mentally retarded children. *Indian Pediatrics,* 5 (5): 209-217.
24. Anand, J.S., and Patel, S.C., 1983, Prevalence and patterns of handicaps in urban centers. *Indian Pediatrics,* 20 (6): 434-438.
25. Anand, M., and Sen, A.K., 1979, Rehearsal strategies in short term memory among retardates and normals. *Indian Journal of Psychology,* 54 (1&2): 33-42.
26. Anandaraj, M.P.J.S., 1987, Probing the Duchenne muscular dystrophy gene. *Bulletin of Human Genetics,* 12 (1):7-8.

27. Ananth, S.S., 1969, The use of operant conditioning with the mental retardates: A report of a pilot experiment. *Indian Journal of Applied Psychology,* 6 (1): 15-21.

28. Anasuya, A., and Rao, B.S.N., 1966, Urinary excretion of hydroxyproline in kwashiorkor. *Indian Journal of Medical Research,* 54 (9): 849-857.

29. Aniah, U., Kumaraiah, V., and Mishra, H., 1991, Behaviour modification in self help skills of mentally retarded children. *Journal of Personality and Clinical Studies,* 7 (1): 15-19.

30. Annamalai, A., Shreekumar, S., and Vellayan, P., 1965, Incidence of juvenile thyrotoxicosis in Madras 1959-1964. *Indian Journal of Pediatrics,* 32 (212): 294-300.

31. Arora, N.K., Singh, M., Paul, V.K., and Bhargava, V.L., 1987, Etiology of foetal growth retardation in hospital born infants. *Indian Journal of Medical Research,* 76 (4): 395-400.

32. Arya, S., 1987, Developmental screening of preschool children: An overview. *Indian Journal of Disability and Rehabilitation,* 2 7-22.

33. Arya, S., 1991, Screening of preschool children for early identification of developmental disabilities in rural areas. *Indian Journal of Clinical Psychology,* 18 (2): 65-70.

34. Arya, S.C., 1970, Information: Education of parents. *Indian Journal of Mental Retardation,* 3 (1): 5-10.

35. Athale, V.H., Nair, R., Kadam, P., Pai, S.K., and Advani, S.H., 1990, Acute lukemia in Down's syndrome. *Indian Pediatrics,* 27 (1): 73-75.

36. Athavale, V.B., 1962, Subdural effusions in pyogenic meningitis in children. *Indian Journal of Child Health,* 11 (11): 572-576.

37. Awasthi, A., Murthy, R.S., Jaloha, R.C., and Pershad, D., 1983, Prevalence study and early identification of mental retardation in rural children: A community based model. *Child Psychiatry Quarterly,* 16 (3): 123-134.

38. Awasthi, A., Murthy, R.S., Jaloha. R.C., and Pershad, D., 1983, Prevalence study and early identification of mental retardation in rural children: A community based model. *Indian Journal of Clinical Psychology,* 10 (2): 263-274.

39. Ayesha, Q., and Malati, T., 1985, Serum protein and immunoglobulins in Duchenne muscular dystrophy. *Indian Journal of Medical Research,* 74 (12): 548-550.

40. Babusenan, G., 1969, Pattern of disability in Ulloor panchayat of Kerala. *The Indian Journal of Social Work,* 29 (4): 411-415.

41. Babusenan, G., 1987, Parental counselling in the rehabilitation of mentally deficient. *Social Welfare*, 34 (1): 4-5.
42. Babusenan, G., and Menon, P.B.M., 1971, Assessment of the problems of the handicapped in a Kerala suburb. *The Journal of Rehabilitation in Asia,* 12 (4): 15-20.
43. Bagchi, R., 1983, Holistic approach as employed in helping a handicapped adult. *Mental Health Review*, 2 (1): 15-17.
44. Bajpai, P.C., and Misra, P.K.,1972 Follow up studies in infantile tremor syndrome. *Indian Journal of Medical Research,* 60 (11): 1711-1717.
45. Bajpai, P.C., Misra, P.K., Tandon, P.N., Nigam, G.J., Vohra, V.C., and Malviya, A., 1968, Serum vitamin B_{12} in infantile tremor syndrome. *Indian Journal of Medical Research,* 56 (8): 1398.
46. Bajpai, P.C., Misra, P.K., Tandon, P.N., Wahal, K.M., and Newton, G., 1969, Infantile tremor syndrome. *Indian Pediatrics,* 6 249.
47. Bajpai, P.C., Misra, P.K., Tandon, P.N., Wahal, K.M., and Newton, G., 1971, Brain biopsy in infantile tremor syndrome. *Indian Journal of Medical Research,* 59 (3): 413-418.
48. Bajpai, P.C., Misra, P.K., and Tandon, P.N., 1968, Further observations on infantile tremor syndrome. *Indian Pediatrics,* 5 297-307.
49. Bajpai, P.C., Tripathi, T.K., Teotia, M., and Saxena, K.C., 1971, Galactosemia: A clinical and enzymological study in a family. *Indian Journal of Pediatrics,* 38 (287): 449-454.
50. Bal, S., 1987, Effects of white noise on reaction in retardate and non retardate children. *Journal of Personality and Clinical Studies,* 3 (2): 95-101.
51. Balachandra, S., 1979, The value of sports and recreation for the mentally retarded. *The Nursing Journal of India,* 20, 3.
52. Balchandani, R.H., 1986, The Disabled: Handicapped. *The Journal of Rehabilitation in Asia,* 27 (3): 12.
53. Bandi, S.K., 1972, Congenital malformations. *Indian Journal of Pediatrics,* 39 (288): 24-29.
54. Banerjee, G., 1975, Another calendar calculator. *Indian Journal of Psychiatry,* 17 (2): 144-146.
55. Banerjee, G.R., 1955, Care of the mentally retarded. *The Indian Journal of Social Work,* 16 (2): 75-82.
56. Banerjee, S., 1982, Psychoanalytic approach to the mentally handicapped. *Samiksha,* 36 (1): 3-12.
57. Banerjee, T.K., 1982, Mentally handicapped: Medico viewpoints.

Samiksha, 36 (1): 18-25.

58. Banerji, B.S., 1970, Investigation about the relationship and interaction patterns of selected pairs of mentally retarded children at "Sharda". *The Journal of Rehabilitation in Asia,* 11: 41-44.

59. Banerji, B.S., 1973, Prevention of mental retardation. *Indian Journal of Mental Retardation,* 6 (1): 33-42.

60. Banerji, B.S., Misra, A.K., and Singh, S.N., 1973, Social relationship of the mentally retarded. *Indian Journal of Mental Retardation,* 6 (2): 81-96.

61. Bansal, P.C., Vare, A.M., and Indurkar, G.M., 1965, Anencephalic monsters: Report of gross anatomical features in five cases. *Indian Journal of Pediatrics,* 32 (209): 197-201.

62. Baru, R.V., 1989, Rehabilitation of disabled children: Lessons from two community projects. *The Indian Journal of Social Work,* 50 (2): 227-233.

63. Barucha, P.E., Iyer, C.G.S., Barucha, E.P., and Deshpande, D.H., 1969, Tuberculous meningitis in children: A clinico pathological evaluation of 24 cases. *Indian Pediatrics,* 6 : 282.

64. Basu, D., 1983, Nursing care of mentally retarded children. *The Nursing Journal of India,* 74 (1): 9-13.

65. Basu, S.N., 1979, The handicapped child in school. *Indian Journal of Pediatrics,* 46 (377): 207-209.

66. Bawa, Y.S., and Wahi, P.L., 1961, Tuberculous meningitis. *Journal of Indian Medical Association,* 37 : 449.

67. Behera, S.K., and Pali, G.B., 1979, Magnesium level of serum and cerebral spinal fluid in cases of protein calorie malnutrition. *Indian Journal of Pediatrics,* 46 (379): 283-288.

68. Behere, P.B., and Tripathi, R.K., 1981, SociodemogRaohic and clinical characteristics of the mentally retarded. *Indian Journal of Mental Retardation,* 14 (1): 1-5.

69. Benkappa, D.G., Prasad, S.R., Sastry, N.S.C., and George, S., 1983, Acute encephalophathy syndrome in Bangalore. *Indian Pediatrics,* 20 (2): 121-127.

70. Bhagat, A., Prasad, A., and Padankatti, B.S., 1983, Learning through recreation: An experiential report with the mentally retarded. *NIMHANS Journal,* 9 (2): 115-118.

71. Bhagvan, R.K., Prasanna, H.A., Shurpalekar, S.R., Chadrasekhara, M.R., Acharya, U.S.V., Swaminathan, M., and Krupanidhi, I., 1964, The use of infant food formulations based on full fat soya flour and peanut protein isolate in the treatment of protein malnutrition,kwashiorkor, *Indian Pediatrics,* 1 (6): 211-214.

72. Bhakop, O.N., Kaur, S., Narang, A., and Verma, S.K., 1977, A longitudinal study of variations in developmental quotients in the first 30 months of life. *Indian Journal of Clinical Psychology*, 4 (1): 59-68.

73. Bhakop, O.N., Walia, B.N.S., and Paulose, P.I., 1963, Galactosemia. *Indian Journal of Pediatrics*, 30 : 87-90.

74. Bhalla, J.N., Bhalla, M., and Tandon, S., 1979, A study of babies delivered by breech presentation. *Indian Journal of Pediatrics*, 46 (381): 353-357.

75. Bhalla, P., and Sen, A.K., 1975, Transfer of learning in retarded and normal children. *Indian Journal of Mental Retardation*, 8 (1): 3-7.

76. Bhandari, B., Singh, R.N., and Shrimati, L.N., 1967, Gonadial dysgenesis, Turner's syndrome, *Indian Journal of Pediatrics*; 34 (235): 292-295.

77. Bhansali, K.M., Mathur, G.M., and Sharma, R., 1979, A study of morbidity patterns in preschool children. *Indian Journal of Pediatrics*, 46 (372): 13-24.

78. Bharatraj, J., 1968, A observational report of four microcephalics in the same family. *Indian Journal of Mental Retardation*, 1 (2): 95-97.

79. Bharatraj, J., 1971, AIISH norms on Seguin Form Board with Indian children. *The Journal of the All India Institute of Speech and Hearing*, 2 : 34-39.

80. Bharatraj, J., 1971, An exploratory study of prevalence of mental retardation in Mysore city. *The Journal of the All India Institute of Speech and Hearing*, 2 : 117-127.

81. Bharatraj, J., 1981, Speech and hearing problems among the mentally retarded. *The Journal of the All India Institute of Speech and Hearing*, 12 : 52-56.

82. Bharatraj, J., 1987, Speech and hearing problems among the mentally retarded. *Indian Journal of Disability and Rehabilitation*, 1 : 5-8.

83. Bhargava, K.S., Sachdev, H.P.S., and Ghosh, S., 1985, Distribution of live births and early neonatal mortality in relation to gestation and intrauterine growths. *Indian Journal of Medical Research*, 74 (7): 95-97.

84. Bhargava, S., and Bhargava, S.K., 1971, Survival growth and development in babies weighting 2000 grams or less. *Indian Pediatrics*, 8 : 1.

85. Bhargava, S.K., Bhargava, V., Kumari, S., Madhavan, S., and

Ghosh, S., 1973, Birth weight gestational age and maternal factors in low birth weight babies. *Indian Pediatrics,* 10 : 161.

86. Bhargava, S.K., Bhargava, V., Kumari, S., Madhavan, S., and Ghosh, S., 1974, Outcome of babies with severe intrauterine growth retardation I: Maternal factors, congenital malformations, mortality and survival pattern. *Indian Journal of Medical Research,* 62 (2): 367.

87. Bhargava, S.K., Bhargava, V., Kumari, S., Madhavan, S., and Ghosh, S., 1976, Babies with severe intrauterine growth retardation: Linear physical growth from 0-24 months. *Indian Journal of Medical Research,* 64 (10): 1480-1485.

88. Bhargava, S.K., Bhargava. V., Tanuja, S., and Ghosh, S., 1971, Birth weight, gestational age and growth patterns of babies with birth weight of 2 kilograms or less. *Indian Pediatrics,* 8 p, 736.

89. Bhargava, S.K., Datta, I., and Kumari, S., 1982, A longitudinal study of language development in small for dates children from birth to five years. *Indian Pediatrics,* 19 (2): 123-129.

90. Bhargava, S.K., Ghosh, S., Lal, U.B., Kumar, A., and Kumari, S., 1974, Morbidity patterns in newborns by gestation and intrauterine growth. Indian Pediatrics, 11 p, 481-485.

91. Bhargava, S.K., Kumari, S., Pandit, N., Prabhakar, A.K., Lamba, M.S., Ghosh, S., and Nanda, S., 1975, Outcome of low birth weight children: A longitudinal study of survival, growth and development from birth to six years. *Indian Academy of Medical Sciences,* 11: 77-99.

92. Bhargava, S.K., and Kishan, J., 1980, Low birth weight and its sequealae: The Indian experience. *Indian Journal of Pediatrics,* 47 (385): 117-121.

93. Bhargava, V., Bhargava, S.K., Kumari, S., and Ghosh, S., 1972, Growth patterns in babies of extreme low birth weight. *Indian Journal of Medical Research,* 60 (10): 1492-1497.

94. Bhargava, V., Ghosh, S., and Bhargava, S.K., 1970, Survival, growth and development in babies weighing 2 kilograms or less. *Indian Pediatrics,* 7 p, 139.

95. Bharucha, M.P.E., 1977, Screening methods for mental retardation: Results of surveys carried out in India. *Indian Pediatrics,* 14 : 395.

96. Bhaskaran, P., Satyanarayana, K., Sivaprasad, J., Jagdeesan, V., Naidu, A.N., and Reddy, V., 1980, Effect of growth retardation in early life on immuno competence in later life. Indian Journal of Medical Research, 69 (10): 519-526.

97. Bhat, B.V., Usha, T.S., Powrany, A., Puri, R.K., Srinivasan, S.,

and Mitra, S.C., 1989, Edwards syndrome with multiple chromosomal effects. *Indian Journal of Pediatrics,* 56 (1): 137-140.

98. Bhatia, B.D., 1964, Helping mentally retarded 1: Counselling the parents of the mentally retarded children. *The Nursing Journal of India,* 45 (6): 165-167.

99. Bhatia, B.D., 1964, Helping mentally retarded 2: Counselling the parents of the mentally retarded children. *The Nursing Journal of India,* 45 (8): 233-234.

100. Bhatia, B.D., Agarwal, K.N., and Jain, N.P., 1983, Muscle mass of intrauterine growth retarded babies in first five months of life. *Indian Pediatrics,* 20 : 671-676.

101. Bhatia, B.D., Agarwal, K.N., and Jain, N.P., 1990, Developmental assessment of intrauterine growth retarded babies of varying maternal aetiology. *Indian Journal of Pediatrics,* 57 (1): 90-104.

102. Bhatia, B.D., Bhargava, V., and Chatterjee, M., 1981, Studies on foetal growth patterns I: Intrauterine growth percentile for singleton liveborn babies. *Indian Pediatrics,* 18 : 647-653.

103. Bhatia, S., Verma, I.C., and Srivastava, S., 1992, Congenital heart disease in Down's syndrome An echocardiograohic study. *Indian Pediatrics,* 29 (9): 1113-1118.

104. Bhattacharyya, A.K., Chattopadhyay, P.S., Roy, P.K., Piladhi., Ganguli, S., and Bhattacharyya, N., 1990, Kwashiorkor and marasmus: Changing hospital incidence of syndrome presentation, 1957-88, *Indian Pediatrics,* 27 (11): 1191-1200.

105. Bhatti, R.S., Channabasavanna, S.M., and Prabhu, L.R., 1985, A tool to study the attitudes of parents towards the management of mentally retarded children. *Child Psychiatry Quarterly,* 18 : 35-43.

106. Bhavani, A.D., 1986, The exceptional in schools. *Mind,* 12 (2): 11-14.

107. Bhogaonkar, A., Sagar, K.B., and Bhakoo, P.N. , 1967, Pierre Robin syndrome. *Indian Journal of Pediatrics,* 34 (236): 332-334.

108. Bhoota, K., 1947, Educating the mentally retarded. *The Indian Journal of Social Work,* 8 (1): 20-26.

109. Bhuvsar, H., 1991, Home bound training programmes. *Mental Health Review,* 5 (2): 23-24.

110. Biswas, M., 1975, Birth order and mental retardation. *Indian Journal of Clinical Psychology,* 2 (2): 73-74.

111. Biswas, M., 1976, Mental retardation as a psychiatric and sociological problem. *Child Psychiatry Quarterly,* 9 (1): 26-27.

112. Boi, G.K., 1972, General and specific problems of preadolescence and adolescent retardates in Sharda. *Special Education in India,* 1 : 27.

113. Bordoloi, B.C., 1979, A humane approach to subnormality. Manosamiksha: *Journal of Gawhati Mental Welfare Society,* 1 (1): 8-10.

114. Borikar, A M., 1976, Work evaluation method for the assessment of vocational potentials in mentally retarded youth. *Indian Journal of Occupational Therapy,* 4 (1): 20-27.

115. Bose, S.K., 1963, Handicapped child, Editorial, *Indian Journal of Child Health,* 12 (12): 809-810.

116. Bose, S.K., 1964, Phenylketonuria, Editorial, *Indian Pediatrics,* 1 (11): 461.

117. Bose, S.K., 1965, Dietary treatment of kwashiorkor. *Indian Pediatrics,* 2 (3): 103-104.

118. Boudnik, I.M., 1962, Differential diagnosis of tuberculous meningitis in children. *Indian Journal of Child Health,* 11 (11): 582-584.

119. Buch, M.B., 1969, Survey of the mentally subnormal children in greater Bombay: St Xaviers Institute of Education. *Guidance and Counselling,* 219 : 204.

120. Campbell, C.M., 1981, Puppetry as an aid in treatment and training. *The Journal of Rehabilitation in Asia,* 22 (2): 29-32.

121. Centerwall, W.R., 1965, The schools, homes and institutions for the mentally retarded in India. *Indian Pediatrics,* 2 (3): 125-132.

122. Centerwall, W.R., Rebellow, P.F., and Kamath, K.R., 1965, Phenylketonuria: A follow up. *Indian Pediatrics,* 2 (11): 417-418.

123. Centerwall, W.R., and Centerwall, S.A., 1966, Consanguinity and congenital anomalies in south India: A pilot study. *Indian Journal of Medical Research,* 54 (12): 1160-1167.

124. Centerwall, W.R., and Kapur, S., 1964, Phenylketonuria. *Indian Pediatrics,* 1 (11): 449-454.

125. Chakrabarty, M.S., Das, B.C., Gupta, B., and Sarkar, J.K., 1975, Rubella as an etiological factor of congenital malformations in Calcutta: A serological study. *Indian Journal of Medical Research,* 63 (10): 1438-1445.

126. Champakam, S., Srikanta, S.C., and Gopalan, G., 1968, Kwashiorkor and mental development. *Journal of Clinical Nutrition,* 21 : 844-852.

127. Chandra, P., Thirupuram, S., and Raju, B.V., 1968, Phenylketonuria in Madras. *Indian Pediatrics,* 5 : 209-211.

128. Chandra, R.K., 1965, Nuclear lobe count and incidence of drumsticks in Indian children with Down's syndrome. *Indian Journal of Pediatrics,* 32 (212): 283-284.

129. Chandra, R.K.,1965, Sequelae of tuberculous meningitis. *Indian Journal of Pediatrics,* 32 (214): 370-371.

130. Chandra, R.K., 1966, Annotations: Expanded Rubella syndrome. *Indian Journal of Pediatrics,* 33 (219): 196-198.

131. Chandrasekaran, R., 1974, Galactosemia: A short communication. *Indian Journal of Mental Retardation,* 7 (2): 98-102.

132. Channabasavanna, S.M., Bhatti, R.S., and Prabhu, L.R., 1985, A study of attitudes of parents towards the management of mentally retarded children. *Child Psychiatry Quarterly,* 18 : 44-47.

133. Char, S.V., 1967, Rehabilitation of the mentally retarded. *Social Welfare,* 14 : 10.

134. Char, S.V., 1970, Training of the mentally retarded. *Swasth Hind,* 14 : 340.

135. Char, S.V., 1972, Primary education for mentally retarded children. *Special Education in India,* 1 (1): 18-19.

136. Chari, T.V.R., 1983, Employment and self employment for needy women and the handicapped. *Social Welfare,* 30 (3): 8.

137. Chattopadhyay, P.K., 1982, Training and education of mentally retarded children: Parent involvement. *Society and Medicine,* 11: 5.

138. Chattopadhyay, P.K., 1982, Training and education of mentally retarded children: Problems of assessment. *Society and Medicine,* 11 : 9.

139. Chattopadhyay, P.K., Bhattacharya, A.K., Roy, A.R., and Biswas, P.K., 1979, Skin conductance and spontaneous autonomic activity in mild mentally retarded children. *Indian Journal of Mental Retardation,* 12 (1&2): 1-5.

140. Chattopadhyay, P.K., Bhattacharya, A.K., Roy, A.R., and Biswas, P.K., 1980, Skin conductance and spontaneous autonomic activity in moderately mentally retarded children. *Indian Journal of Mental Retardation,* 13 : 24.

141. Chattopadhyay, P.K., Roy, A.R., Biswas, P.K., and Bhattacharya, A.K., 1980, Interrelations between latency amplitude and rise time of the Galvanic Skin Response in severely mentally retarded child. *Child Psychiatry Quarterly,* 13 (3): 72-77.

142. Chattopadhyay, P.K., Roy, A.R., Biswas, P.K., and Bhattacharya, A.K., 1979, Spontaneous autonomic activity in severely mentally retarded children. *Child Psychiatry Quarterly,* 12 (3): 57-60.

143. Chattopadhyay, P.K., Roy, A.R., Biswas, P.K., and Bhattacharya,

A.K., 1980, A study of arousal in mentally retarded children. *Indian Journal of Clinical Psychology,* 7 (1): 47-52.

144. Chattopadhyay, P.K., Roy, A.R., and Bhattacharya, A.K., 1980, Skin conductance recovery limb in severely mentally retarded children. *Indian Journal of Clinical Psychology,* 7 (1): 53-58.

145. Chattopadhyay, P.K., and Bhattacharya, A.K., 1980, IQ on two tests: A correlational study with mentally retarded children. *Child Psychiatry Quarterly,* 13 (3): 78-80.

146. Chaturvedi, S.K., and Malhotra, S., 1982, Treatment seeking behaviour of parents of mentally retarded children. *Indian Journal of Clinical Psychology,* 9 (2): 211-216.

147. Chaturvedi, S.K., and Malhotra, S., 1983, Parental attitudes towards mental retardation. *Child Psychiatry Quarterly,* 16 (3): 135-142.

148. Chaturvedi, S.K., and Malhotra, S., 1984, A follow up study of mental retardation focusing on parental attitudes. *Indian Journal of Psychiatry,* 26 (4): 370-376.

149. Chaturvedi, S.K., and Malhotra, S., 1988, Psychiatric problems in mental retardation. *Child Psychiatry Quarterly,* 21 (3): 96-101.

150. Chaudhuri, A., 1960, Aminoacids and nutritional dystrophy, Editorial, *Indian Journal of Pediatrics,* 27 (154): 408.

151. Chaudhuri, A., 1964, The chromosomes: An introduction with some observations in Indian children. *Indian Journal of Pediatrics,* 31 (197): 175-186.

152. Chaudhuri, A., Basu, S.N., and Chatterjee, M., 1970, 46 XY -G +t,Gq Gq, Karyptype in a mongol. *Indian Journal of Pediatrics,* 37 : 469.

153. Chaudhuri, A., Patil, S., and Chaudhuri, K.C., 1966, G_{21}/G translocation chromosome in a boy with mongolism. *Indian Journal of Pediatrics,* 33 (224): 288-292.

154. Chaudhuri, A., and Chaudhuri, K.C., 1966, Clinical and cytogenetic findings in 20 patients with mongolism. *Indian Journal of Pediatrics,* 33 (224): 298-306.

155. Chaudhuri, K.C., and Misra, R.P., 1960, Pattern of amino acid excretion in urine of dystrophic children,nutritional dystrophy, *Indian Journal of Pediatrics,* 27 (154): 389-394.

156. Chaudhuri, R.K., 1967, Intra uterine growth retardation, Annotations, *Indian Journal of Pediatrics,* 34 (233): 218-219.

157. Chaudhuri, R.K., 1967, Minimal brain damage syndrome, Annotations, *Indian Journal of Pediatrics,* 34 (231): 151-152.

158. Chaudhuri, S., 1986, Psychosocial characteristics of the handicapped children. *Indian Journal of Pediatrics*, 53 (2): 229-236.

159. Chaudhuri, S., Shide, S.V., Barve, S.S., Dixit, H.S., and Pandit, A., 1990, A longitudinal follow up of neurodevelopment of high risk newborns: A comparison of Amrel-Tison's method with Bayley Scales of Infant Development. *Indian Pediatrics*, 27 (8): 799-802.

160. Chawla, P.L., and Neki, J.S., 1978, Mental retardation: A study of parents "appreciative ability" and experiences. *Journal of the All India Institute of Medical Sciences*, 3 (1): 87-96.

161. Chhabria, B., 1984, Development of talent among handicap and their integration with cultural activities of the societies: Report on a workshop. *The Journal of Rehabilitation in Asia*, 25 (1): 52-54.

162. Chhaparwal, B.L., Singh, S.D., Mehta, S., and Pohowalla, J.N., 1971 Magnesium levels in serum and CSF in meningo-encephalitic syndrome,Tremor syndrome, *Indian Journal of Pediatrics*, 38 (282): 331-333.

163. Chhaparwal, B.L., and Pohowalla, J.N., 1966, Magnesium levels in serum and in CSF in common neurological disorders in infants and children. *Indian Pediatrics*, 3 p 139.

164. Chitre, V.S., Santhagopalan, T., Ramanathan, M.K., and Balasubramanyam, M., 1962, Some observations on the serum copper and paRaohenylene diamine oxidase PPD-oxidase copper oxidase activity in nutritional oedema syndrome, kwashiorkor, *Indian Journal of Pathology and Bacteria*, S, 2 : 93-96.

165. Chitre, V.S., and Balasubramanyam, M., 1969, Changes in serum copper and PPD oxidase in different diseases, Part I: Differential observation in certain types of leprosy and kwashiorkor. *Indian Journal of Medical Research*, 57 (2): 228-236.

166. Choksi, K., 1991, An anecdotal account of my experiences with adolescent and adult mentally retarded at the BM Institute of Mental Health. *Mental Health Review*, 5 (2): 45-46.

167. Chopra, H.D., 1973, Treatment of encopresis in a mongol with operant conditioning. *Indian Journal of Mental Retardation*, 6 (2): 43-46.

168. Chouhan, V.L., and Ibrahim, I., 1989, Behavioural peculiarities of disabled children. *DEI Research Journal of Education and Psychology*, 9 (1): 21-24.

169. Colaco M.P., Desai, M.P., and Ajgaonkar, A.R., 1984, Neonatal

screening for hypothyroidism. *Indian Pediatrics,* 21 p 695-700.

170. Cornelius, D.J.K., 1972, A program for industrial training and employment of the mentally retarded. *The Journal of Rehabilitation in Asia,* 13 (3): 33.

171. Cornelius, D.J.K., 1974, Training of the mentally retarded. *The Journal of Rehabilitation in Asia,* 15 (3): 4-9.

172. Cornelius, D.J.K., 1989, Restructure of the work environment for the mentally retarded persons. *Indian Journal of Disability and Rehabilitation,* 3 (2): 81-84.

173. Crasta, L.F.I., 1973, Simple nursing techniques of premature babies. *The Nursing Journal of India,* 54 (3): 81-82/93.

174. Dadu, J., 1982, A study of parent participation of young developmentally handicapped children. *Mental Health Review,* 1 (1): 110-114.

175. Damle, S.G., 1952, Background study of the mentally retarded children in Tata Institute of Social Sciences,TISS, Bombay. *The Indian Journal of Social Work,* 10 p 11-13.

176. Damle, S.G., 1952, Mentally retarded children. *The Indian Journal of Social Work,* 13 (3): 153-161.

177. Das, J.P., 1968, Cultural deprivation. *Indian Journal of Mental Retardation,* 1 (1): 1-3.

178. Das, J.P., 1973, How to teach retardates to control their behaviour. *Indian Journal of Mental Retardation,* 6 (1): 5-20.

179. Das, J.P., and Orn, D.E., 1972, BiogRaohical characteristics and socio economic status of children below IQ 100. *Indian Journal of Mental Retardation,* 5 : 3-17.

180. Das, J.P., and Pivato E., 1977, Effect of malnutrition on cognitive competence. *Indian Journal of Mental Retardation,* 10 (1): 1-23.

181. Das, S.S., 1958, Gustatory perception of mentally deficients. *Indian Journal of Psychology,* 33 : 177-182.

182. Dasgupta, J., 1973, Cytogenetic anomalies in cases seen at Pondicherry. *Indian Journal of Medical Research,* 61 (1): 62-70.

183. Dasgupta, J.C., 1948, Social adjustment of the mentally deficient children. *The Indian Journal of Social Work,* 9 (2): 105-111.

184. Dastur, D.K., Manghani, D.K., Joshi, M.K., and Adavi, S.V., 1966, Maole Syrup Urine Disease in Indian baby: Brachid chain amino and ketoaciduria. *Indian Journal of Medical Research,* 54 (10): 415-422.

185. Date, S., 1986, Parent training for the care of the mentally retarded. *Community Mental Health News,* 7 (1): 3-4.

186. Datta, D., 1987, Down's syndrome: A comparative study of

aetiological variables. *Child Psychiatry Quarterly,* 20 (2): 43-48.

187. Datta, J., 1987, Learning ability of mentally retarded children and the errors they commit. *Indian Journal of Disability and Rehabilitation,* 2 : 23-29.

188. Datta, T., 1981, Mental retardation as a function of cognitive incompetence: Some socio-cultural variables involved in this relationship. *Indian Journal of Mental Retardation,* 14 (2): 47-55.

189. Dattabanik, N.D., 1978, A study of different birth weight babies and related factors. *Indian Pediatrics,* 15 : 327-334.

190. Dattabanik, N.D., Krishna, R., Mane, S.I.S., and Lala, R., 1967, Longitudinal study on morbidity and mortality pattern of children in Delhi during the first two years of life. *Indian Journal of Medical Research,* 55 (3): 504.

191. Dave, U., Chauhan, V., and Dalvi, J., 1991, Evaluation of mental in cognitive and behavioural dysfunction of mentally retarded children : A placebo controlled study. *Probe,* 30 (3): 240-246.

192. Dave, U.P., 1990, Enhancement of adaptability of mentally retarded children. *Disabilities and Impairments,* 4 (1): 45-50.

193. David, S., 1984, Prevention, early detection and timely intervention of disabilities in preschool children. *Mental Health Review,* 2 (2): 23-25.

194. David, S., and Apte, S.R., 1991, Methods and importance of early intervention programme. *Mental Health Review,* 5 (2) : 3-15.

195. Dayal, R.S., Lahari, B., Halder, P.K., Kehar, V., Prasad, R., Mathur, G.P., and Wahi, P.N., 1962, Gargoylism. *Indian Journal of Pediatrics,* 29 (170): 65-68.

196. Dayal, R.S., Prasad, R., and Mathur, G.P., 1961, Galactosemia: An interesting case of survival. *Indian Journal of Pediatrics,* 28: 429.

197. Deb, S., 1958, Perception of mental deficients. *Indian Journal of Psychology,* 33 : 171-182.

198. Deb, S., 1964, Immediate memory span: Brain injured and familial imbeciles. *Indian Journal of Psychology,* 39 : 91-94.

199. Deb, S., 1966, Management of the mentally retarded: An overview. Bulletin of Council for Social and Psychological Research, 7 : 21.

200. Deb, S., 1982, Functional aspects of handicapped education. *Indian Journal of Mental Retardation,* 15 (1): 35-37.

201. Deb, S., and Ghose, R., 1962, Roles of cultural background on the recognition of culture based objects by a group of moderately mentally retarded subjects. *Indian Journal of Psychology,* 37 : 181-184.

202. Deivasigamani, T.R., 1990, Psychiatric morbidity in primary school children: An epidemiological study. *Indian Journal of Psychiatry,* 32 (3): 235-240.

203. Deodhar, N.S., 1968, Maternal rubella and the risk of congenital malformation in infants: A review. *Indian Journal of Public Health,* 12 (3): 140-148.

204. Desai, N.S., and Cunningham, M.D., 1986, Follow up of low birth weight infants. *Indian Journal of Pediatrics,* 53 (3): 373-384.

205. Desai, P., 1989, Individualised instruction. *Journal of Indian Education,* 14, (1): 32-35.

206. Deshpande, S.N., and Mathur, M.N.L., 1990, Factors in mental retardation. *Indian Journal of Disability and Rehabilitation,* 4 (2): 53-54.

207. Deshpande, S.N., and Mathur, M.N.L., 1991, Birth order and mental retardation. *Indian Journal of Disability and Rehabilitation,* 5 (2): 13-16.

208. Deshpande, T.V., and Hinton, G.G., 1981, Intrauterine growth retardation and its impact on the neurological status of the new born. *Indian Journal of Pediatrics,* 48 : 305-310.

209. Deshpande, T.V., and Ingle, V.N., 1969, Tremor syndrome in children. *Indian Pediatrics,* 6 : 550.

210. Desousa, A., and Desousa, D.A., 1976, Psuedo-mental retardation. *Child Psychiatry Quarterly,* 9 (4): 1-5

211. Desousa, A., and Iyer, D.S., 1969, Mental deficiency: An analysis of 100 cases. *Child Psychiatry Quarterly,* 2 : 5-11.

212. Desousa, D.A., 1979, Parent counselling. *Community Psychiatry Journal,* 5 (2): 29-30.

213. Devadiga, K.V., 1975, Head injury in children. *Indian Journal of Pediatrics,* 42 (333): 291-297.

214. Devanath, R., 1979, The disabled child. *Journal of Indian Medical Association,* 73 (7&8): 134-135.

215. Devi, A.V.S., 1976, Short communication on parental attitudes towards retarded children. *Child Psychiatry Quarterly,* 9 (2): 10-12.

216. Devi, N.S., 1958, Perinatal anoxia. *Indian Journal of Pediatrics,* 25 (126): 417-421.

217. Devi, S., Mathur, M.N.L., and Dayal, S., 1980, Incidence of mental retardation in a Child Guidance Clinic. *Indian Journal of Mental Retardation,* 13 : 43-47.

218. Dhar, B.N., 1967, Plea for the mentally retarded. *Social Welfare,* 14 : 6.

219. Dharitri, R., and Murthy, V N., 1987, Handicapped children: Their abilities and behaviour. *Indian Journal of Clinical Psychology,* 14 (1): 12-17.

220. Dhiman, S.R., 1987, Total protien and mental retardation: A quantitative approach. *Disabilities and Impairments,* 1 (1&2): 1-8.

221. Dhiman, S.R., Sethi, S., and Sethi, P.K., 1992, Serum albumins in individuals with mental handicap. *Disabilities and Impairments,* 4 (1&2): 72-80.

222. Dikshit, A.K., 1957, Nutritional dystrophy and anemia. *Indian Journal of Child Health,* 6 (3): 132.

223. Dikshit, K.D., and Agrawal, B.D., 1960, Galactosemia: A case report. *Indian Journal of Child Health,* 9 (10): 542.

224. Dosagh, N.L., 1969, Impact of counselling on a mentally handicapped. *Indian Journal of Mental Retardation,* 2 (2): 34-39.

225. Dubey, B.L., Pershad, D., and Sharma, G.C., 1977, Psychologist and their role in dealing with handicapped in India. *The Journal of Rehabilitation in Asia,* 18 (3): 26-29.

226. Dubey, B.L., and Khanna, S., 1972, A study of hearing and speech defects in mentally retarded children. *Indian Journal of Mental Retardation,* 5 (2): 89-94.

227. Dutt, V., 1987, National Institute for the Mentally Handicapped, NIMH, and Ali Yavar Jung National Institute for the Hearing Handicapped, AYJNIHH, *Indian Journal of Disability and Rehabilitation,* 2 : 31-36.

228. Dutta, D., Das, S., and Talukdar, L.K., 1984, An observation of play in a group of mentally handicapped children. *Child Psychiatry Quarterly,* 17 (3): 94-99.

229. Dutta, T., 1981, Mental retardation as a function of cognitive incompetance: Some socio-cultural variables involved in this relationship. *Indian Journal of Mental Retardation,* 14 : 47.

230. Dwivedi, C.M., 1988, A comparative study on achievement motivation in normal and Down's syndrome children. *Child Psychiatry Quarterly,* 21 (1): 19-22.

231. Easu, D., 1983, Nursing of mentally retarded children. *The Nursing Journal of India,* 65 (1): 9-13.

232. Ember, P., 1979, Workshops for parents of the mentally retarded. *Indian Journal of Mental Retardation,* 12 (1&2): 31-42.

233. Ember, P., Kinker, R., Rudra, R., and Murthy, P., 1979, The effect of activation theRaoy on severely subnormal children. *Indian Journal of Clinical Psychology,* 6 (2): 105-110.

234. Fakhir, S., and Adhami, S., 1990, Acute cerebellar ataxia in enteric fever. *Indian Pediatrics,* 27 (6): 635.

235. Gandhi, J.S., 1968, Inter-learning among hetrogenous groups of mentally retarded. *Indian Journal of Mental Retardation,* 1 (1): 34-37.

236. Gandhi, J.S., 1979, Search of and for the mentally retarded. *Indian Journal of Mental Retardation,* 12 (1&2): 56-62.

237. Gandhi, J.S., and Agrawal, K.G., 1969, Attitude of public towards mental retardation. *Indian Journal of Mental Retardation,* 2 (1): 21-25.

238. Gandhi, J.S., and Cheema, M., 1969, The follow up of the mentally retarded. *Indian Journal of Mental Retardation,* 2 (2): 68-73.

239. Gandotra, V.S., 1985, Management problems and practices of home makers with a disabled member in the family. *The Indian Journal of Social Work,* 45 (4): 484-490.

240. Ganesan, V., 1978, The need for child centered education for the disadvantaged children. *The Journal of Rehabilitation in Asia,* 19 (1): 16-18.

241. Ganguly, C., Ganguly, P., Sarangi, N.N., and Mukherjee, K.L., 1986, Mucopolysaccharidoses in Calcutta. *Indian Journal of Pediatrics,* 53 (2): 263-270.

242. Ganguly, D., 1968, Problems involving social and emotional adjustment among mentally retarded children. *Indian Journal of Mental Retardation,* 1 (1): 29-33.

243. Ganguly, D., 1969, Characteristic developmental parallels and psychomotor correlates of intellectual functioning in mental retardation. *Indian Journal of Experimental Psychology,* 3 (1): 50-53.

244. Ganguly, H.C., 1968, Prevalence of psychological disorders in an Indian industrial population: Part I, II and III. *Indian Journal of Medical Research,* 56, (5): 745-776.

245. Ganguly, H.C., 1969, Mental health study of an Indian industrial population. *The Indian Journal of Social Work,* 30 (2): 123-132.

246. Garg, B.K., 1967, Oxycephaly. *Indian Journal of Pediatrics,* 34 (235): 288-291.

247. Garg, B.K., 1968, Acute cerebellar ataxia following varicella. *Indian Pediatrics,* 5 (5): 230-233.

248. Garg, B.K., 1977, Tuberculous meningitis in children. *Indian Journal of Pediatrics,* 44 (351): 87-91.

249. Garg, B.K., and Srivastava, J.R., 1969, Infantile tremor syndrome. *Indian Journal of Pediatrics,* 36 (257): 213-218.

250. Gautam, U., and Dilip, K.A., 1981, Relationship between comprehensive capacity as assessed by Raven's Progressive Matrices and nutrition as assessed by composite anthropometric indices. *Indian Journal of Mental Retardation,* 14 (1): 6-12.

251. George, E.I., 1975, Management of the educable mentally retarded and of the emotionally disturbed children. *Kerala Journal of Psychiatry,* 3 : 14.

252. George, J., 1964, Mental retardation, psychological factors: A programme of research and rehabilitation. *Transactions of All India Institute for Mental Health,* 4 : 17.

253. Gera, K., Wellington, M., and Purohit, S., 1978, An exploratory study of retardates interaction with mother in a game situation. *Indian Journal of Mental Retardation,* 11 (1): 1-11.

254. Ghafoor, P.K., Abdul, M.I. and Naik, V.P., 1971, Pyrithioxine, Encephabol, in mentally deficient children: A trial on fifty cases. *Antiseptic,* 68 (2): 93-96.

255. Ghai, A., and Sen, A., 1992, A comparative study of the characteristic behaviour of high and low excitable retarded under different game strategies. *Disabilities and Impairments,* 4 (1&2): 62-71.

256. Ghai, O.P., 1975, Effect of early marasmic malnutrition on subsequent mental development. *Indian Pediatrics,* 12 p 85.

257. Ghai, O.P., 1980, Physical and neurodevelopmental handicaps of low birth weight infants. *Indian Journal of Pediatrics,* 47 (386): 233-238.

258. Ghai, O.P., Ratna, K., Ramachandran, K., and Neki, J.S., 1973, Effect of early marasmic malnutrition on subsequent mental development. *Indian Pediatrics,* 10 : 155-158.

259. Ghatak, R., and Indiresan, J., 1983, Family dynamism and performance of educable mentally retarded. *Journal of Psychological Researches,* 27 (2): 66-69.

260. Ghooi, A.M., Khanna, T., and Gupta, M.M., 1976, An analysis of 500 cases of head injury in children. *Indian Journal of Pediatrics,* 43 (342): 191-197.

261. Ghosh, A., 1974, Mental retardation: Historical aspects. *Indian Journal of Mental Retardation,* 7 (2): 86-88.

262. Ghosh, A., and Beri, S., 1962, Standard of prematurity for north Indian babies. *Indian Journal of Child Health,* 11 (5): 210-215.

263. Ghosh, B.N., Dass, N.K., and Haldar, A.K., 1984, Disability prevalence in an urban community in relation to socio-economic conditions. *Indian Journal of Medical Research,* 73 : 347-354.

264. Ghosh, R., 1967, Educating the mentally handicapped: Curriculum for the educables and trainables. *Social Welfare,* 14 : 8.

265. Ghosh, S., 1963, Nialamide in the treatment of mental retardation. *Indian Journal of Child Health,* 12 (6): 347-349.

266. Ghosh, S., Bhargava, S.K., Madhavan, S., Tasker, A.D., Bhargava, V., and Nigam, S.K., 1971, Intrauterine growth of north Indian babies. *Indian Pediatrics,* 8 : 862-830.

267. Ghosh, S., Bhargava, S.L., Beri, S., and Nangia, B.S., 1962, Tuberous sclerosis. *Indian Journal of Child Health,* 11 (12): 633-635.

268. Ghosh, S., Hooja, V., Mittal, S.K., and Varma, R.K., 1977, Biosocial determinants of birth weight. *Indian Pediatrics,* 14 : 107-119.

269. Ghosh, S., and Dagga, S., 1967, Comparison of gestational age and weights as statements of prematurity. Indian Pediatrics, 4 (4): 173.

270. Ghosh, S., and Mohan, M., 1962, Mongolism: A study of fifty cases. *Indian Journal of Child Health,* 11 (11): 563-567.

271. Girimaji, S.R., 1990, Early diagnosis and management of mental retardation. *Indian Journal of Psychological Medicine,* 13 (2): 209-213.

272. Girimaji, S.R., 1993, Family intervention in mental retardation: An overview. *NIMHANS Journal,* 11 (1): 21-26.

273. Girimaji, S.R., Srinath, S., Sheshadri, S., Rao P.M., and Nardev, G., 1990, Pattern of utilisation of outpatient group counselling services for parents of mentally retarded persons. *Indian Journal of Psychological Medicine,* 13 (3): 153-157.

274. Goel, S.K., 1981, Problems in the usage of psychological tests with mentally retarded: A global picture. *Indian Journal of Mental Retardation,* 14 (2): 56-78.

275. Goel, S.K., 1989, Integrated education of mental retardates. *Journal of Indian Education,* 14 (6): 20-28.

276. Goel, S.K., and Sen, A.K., 1981, Psychological assessment of the mentally retarded and evolution of the tests. *Indian Journal of Mental Retardation,* 14 (1): 19-26.

277. Goi, G.K., 1972, General and specific problems of pre-adolescents and adolescent retardates in Sharada. *Special Education in India,* 1 (1): 27-31.

278. Gokhale, S.D., 1968, Programmes for the mentally retarded. *Social Welfare,* 14 : 6-7.

279. Gokhale, S.D., 1982, Rehabilitation of disabled workers in Asia

and Oceana. *The Indian Journal of Social Work,* 33 (1): 27-38.

280. Gopalan, C., 1969, Studies on pathogenesis of some nutritional deficiency states. *Indian Journal of Medical Research,* 57 (8): 75-91.

281. Gopalan, S., and Ramalingaswami, V., 1955, Kwashiorkor in India. *Indian Journal of Medical Research,* 43 (4): 751-773.

282. Gopinath, P.S., Radhakrishnan, V.K., Chaturvedi, S.K., Murali, T., Salim, P.P., and Sarmukudam, S., 1987, Duration of stay and work performance of mentally handicapped in a day care centre. *Indian Journal of Psychiatry,* 29 (2): 149-153.

283. Goswami, P., and Barua, R.K., 1959, Paper electrophoretac protein pattern in nutritional oedema. *Indian Journal of Pediatrics,* 26 (138): 253-257

284. Gour, K.N., 1956, Tuberculous meningitis in children. *Indian Journal of Pediatrics,* 23 (103): 317-320.

285. Goyal, J., and Mittal, A.C., 1976, Small bowel obstruction due to trichobezoar. *Indian Journal of Pediatrics,* 43 (339): 108-110.

286. Goyal, S.C., Tak, S.K., and Bhandari, B., 1989, Determination of gestational age: Comparative accuracy of different methods. *Indian Journal of Pediatrics,* 56 (1): 115-120.

287. Grewal, H.S., Mathur, S., Thapar, R.K., and Agarwal, J.K., 1967, Facioscapulo-humeral muscular dystrophy. *Indian Journal of Pediatrics,* 34 (232): 186-188.

288. Guha, D.K., 1967, Developmental aspects of neurological disorders in infants and children. *Indian Journal of Pediatrics,* 34 (236): 319-324.

289. Guha, D.K., 1967, Developmental aspects of neurological disorders in infants and children. *Indian Journal of Pediatrics,* 34 (237): 360-366.

290. Guha, D.K., 1967, Developmental aspects of neurological disorders in infants and children. *Indian Journal of Pediatrics,* 34 (239): 432-436.

291. Guha, D.K., Rashmi, A., and Kochhar, M., 1970, Birth injuries: Incidence, aetiology, diagnosis and management. *Indian Journal of Pediatrics,* 37 (268): 185-191.

292. Gujral, A., Rao S., Gladstone, B., Nair, C.N., Pai, S.K., Kurkure, P.A., and Advani, S.H., 1993 Down syndrome with Hodgkins disease. *Indian Pediatrics,* 30 (5): 684-689.

293. Gunthey, R.K., and Upadhyaya, S., 1982, Adaptive behaviour in retarded and non retarded children. *Indian Journal of Clinical Psychology,* 9 (2): 163-166.

294. Gunthey, R.K., 1981, Socio-cultural deprivation and adaptive behaviour. *Child Psychiatry Quarterly,* 14 (4): 35-37.

295. Gupta, A., Akre, B.R., and Rawat, M.S., 1967, Trichobezoar. *Indian Pediatrics,* 4 (8): 335-337.

296. Gupta, B.D., Maheswari, R.K., and Miglani, N., 1978, Infantile tremor syndrome. *Indian Journal of Pediatrics,* 45 (366): 221-228.

297. Gupta, B.W., and Mathur, Y.N., 1979, Disadvantaged child. *Swasth Hind,* 23 : 205.

298. Gupta, J.P., 1977, Legislation for the care of mentally retarded in India. *Mental Retardation Digest,* 4 : 14.

299. Gupta, M., and Mukesh, C., 1978, Mental retardation and role of society. *Journal of Rajasthan Psychiatric Society,* 1 (2): 19-22.

300. Gupta, M.C., Thapar, R.K., and Nigam, D.K., 1968, ECG changes in muscular dystrophy. *Indian Journal of Pediatrics,* 35 (242): 131-134.

301. Gupta, R.K., Sen, A.K., and Nath, S., 1978, Differential growth pattern of the mentally retarded: A biometric study. *Indian Journal of Mental Retardation,* 11 (2): 93-108.

302. Gupta, S., Dhingara, D.C., Singh, M.V., and Ananda, N.K., 1975, Impact of nutrition on intelligence. *Indian Pediatrics,* 12 : 1079-1083.

303. Gupta, S., and Singh, M.V., 1973, Marriage and sex education of mental retardates. *Child Psychiatry Quarterly,* 6 : 15-17.

304. Gupta, S.C., 1970, An analysis of 300 mentally retarded cases. *Indian Journal of Mental Retardation,* 3 (1): 69-74.

305. Gupta, S.C., and Sethi, B.B., 1970, Prevalence of mental retardation in Uttar Pradesh. *Indian Journal of Psychiatry,* 12 : 264-272.

306. Gupta, S.K., Sanghi, S., Sharma, U., Acharya, U., and Raman, S., 1990, Precipitation test: Raoid method for diagnosis of tuberculous meningitis. *Indian Pediatrics,* 27 (11): 1183-1186.

307. Gupta, S.P., 1970, Gargoylism in two families from north India. *Indian Journal of Pediatrics,* 37 (265): 69-72.

308. Gupta, S.P., Gupta, P.C., Kumar, V., and Ahuja, M.S.S., 1972, ElectroencephalogRaohic changes in hypothyroidism. *Indian Journal of Medical Research,* 60 (7): 1101-1106.

309. Gurudas, S., 1979, Self-actualisation and rehabilitation. *The Journal of Rehabilitation in Asia,* 20 (3): 21-23.

310. Habibullah, M.I., 1985, Helping the handicapped. *Yojana,* 29 (5): 24.

311. Habibullah, M.I., 1986, On removing disabilities of the handicapped. *Yojana,* 30 (5): 26-28.

312. Habibullah, M.I., 1986, Rehabilitating the handicapped. *Yojana,* 30 (21): 31-33.

313. Hafeez, M.A., and RaajashekaRaopa, M., 1958, Amarautic familial idiocy. *Journal of Indian Medical Association,* 30 : 57.

314. Hariasara, M., 1981, A developmentally handicapped child in the family: Parents perception, attitudes, and their participation in the programme. *Mental Health Review,* 1 (2): 55-60.

315. Hegde, S., 1981, Handicapped children. *The Nursing Journal of India,* 72 (5): 138.

316. Ingle, V.N., 1964, Two cases of galactosemia from Aurangabad. *Indian Pediatrics,* 1 : 58.

317. Ingle, V.N., 1966, Hyperaminoaciduria in childhood. *Indian Journal of Pediatrics,* 33 (217): 56-62.

318. Ingle, V.N., and Mali, V.B., 1970, Cornelia De Lange Syndrome: Report of two cases in siblings. *Indian Journal of Pediatrics,* 37 (267): 149-151.

319. Ishtiaq, K., 1976, Sociological aspects of mental retardation. *Indian Journal of Mental Retardation,* 9 : 77-82.

320. Ishtiaq, K., and Chandra, S., 1981, Mental retardation: A psychological analysis. *Indian Journal of Mental Retardation,* 14: 3-18.

321. Ishtiaq, K., and Chandra, S.,1975, Mental retardation: A psychological analysis. *Indian Journal of Mental Retardation,* 8 (1): 13-18.

322. Ishtiaq, K., and Kamal, S., 1981, A comparative study of the mentally retarded and the blind. *Indian Journal of Mental Retardation,* 14 : 3.

323. Ismail, F., 1960, The handicapped in the nations economy. *The Indian Journal of Social Work,* 21 (4): 102-103.

324. Iyer, K., and Mukul, N., 1990, Infants with disabilities. *Social Change,* 20 (3): 44-50.

325. Iyer, R.S., 1990, Neonatal behavioural assessment. *Indian Pediatrics,* 27 (8): 795-798.

326. Jachuk, K., Datta, T., and Das, J.P., 1968, Age, stimulus, meaningfulness and semantic satiation. *Indian Journal of Mental Retardation,* 1 (1): 20-28.

327. Jachuk, K., and Mohanty, A.K., 1974, Low socio-economic status and progressive retardation in cognitive skills: A test of cumulative

deficit hypothesis. *Indian Journal of Mental Retardation,* 7 (2): 36-45.

328. Jain, M.C., and Satyavati, K., 1969, A preliminary note on the problems in the family with a mentally retarded child. *Transactions of All India Institute for Mental Health,* 9 : 23-29.

329. Jain, M.K., and Shah, M.D., 1993, Hydranencephaly / multicystic encephalomacia: Association with congenital ruebella infection. *Indian Pediatrics,* 30 (2): 253-256.

330. Jain, N., and Kureshi, A., 1992, Concept formation ability among normal and handicapped children: A comparative study. *Journal of Personality and Clinical Studies,* 19 (1 & 2): 37-39.

331. Jain, R., 1981, Asian meeting on childhood disability: Family and community roles. *Social Welfare,* 28 (8): 9.

332. Jain, S.P., and Singh, R.V., 1965, Turner's syndrome. *Indian Journal of Pediatrics,* 32 (207): 128-131.

333. Jangira, N.K., 1987, Education for rehabilitation of the disabled. *Indian Journal of Disability and Rehabilitation,* 1 : 9-12.

334. Jangira, N.K., and Ahuja, A., 1990, Disability and disabled persons in newspapers: A review. *Indian Journal of Disability and Rehabilitation,* 4 (1): 55-70.

335. Jaswal, S., and Jaswal, I.J.S., 1978, Physical growth and mental retardation: A review. *Man in India,* 58 : 240-254.

336. Jaswal, S., and Jaswal, I.J.S., 1981, An anthropometric study of body size in Down syndrome. *Indian Pediatrics,* 18 (1): 81-84.

337. Jaswal, S., and Jaswal, I.J.S., 1984, Anthropometry of mongol males and females. *Indian Pediatrics,* 21 : 299-306.

338. Jaswal, S., and Jaswal, I.J.S., 1988, Malformation of the head in Down syndrome. *Indian Pediatrics,* 25 (4): 373-376.

339. Jaswal, S., and Jaswal, I.J.S., 1984, Dermatoglyphics and mental retardation: A review. *Man in India,* 64 : 203-216.

340. Jayalakshmi, V.T., Ramanathan, M.K., and Gopalan, C., 1957, Some observation on effects of treatment of cases of kwashiorkor. *Indian Journal of Medical Research,* 45 (3): 431-438.

341. Jayaram, M., 1974, Is the concept of mental retardation apt? : A critical discussion. *Journal of All India Institute for Speech and Hearing,* 5 (6): 72-78.

342. JayashankaRaopa, B.S., 1986, Intellectual tests and social adaptive behavioural scales used for the assessment of the mentally handicapped in India. *Journal of Personality and Clinical Studies,* 2 (2): 89-98.

343. JayashankaRaopa, B.S., and Puri, R.K., 1984, Parental counselling of the mentally retarded children. *Child Psychiatry Quarterly,* 17 (3): 109-112.

344. Jayawardena, H.A., 1977 Handicapped children: Early detection and management. *The Journal of Rehabilitation in Asia,* 18 (4): 21-23.

345. Jehan, Q., and Ansari, A., 1981, A study of certain psychosocial characteristics of mentally retarded children. *Indian Journal of Clinical Psychology,* 8 (1): 47-48.

346. Jehan, Q., and Ansari, Z., 1983, Impact of parental education in the adjustment progress of their mentally retarded children. *Child Psychiatry Quarterly,* 16 : 153.

347. Jesti, D.V., Sule, S.M., Apte, J.S., and Vahia, N.S., 1973, Gilles de la Tourette's Disease: Multiple vocal and motor tics. *Indian Journal of Pediatrics,* 40 (311): 435-438.

348. Jesudason, V., Amujadevi, K.A., and Bhogle, S., 1979, Determinants of motor and mental development during early childhood. *The Indian Journal of Social Work,* 40 (1): 27-40.

349. Jha, S.K., 1976, The mentally backward child. *Indian Journal of Pediatrics,* 43 (341): 178-180.

350. Jiloha, R.C., 1989, The effect of activation theRaoy on severely retarded children. *Indian Journal of Disability and Rehabilitation,* 3 (1): 19-24.

351. Jiloha, R.C., and Murthy, E.C., 1981, An epidemiological study of psychiatric problems in primary school children. *Child Psychiatry Quarterly,* 14 (4): 1-12.

352. Jindal, C.R., 1982, Toward helping the mentally retarded to learn. *Indian Journal of Mental Retardation,* 15 (1): 43-50.

353. Jindal, T., and Chatterjee, A.K., 1980, Trichobezoar and mental retardation. *Indian Journal of Psychiatry,* 22 (2): 213.

354. John, T.J., Date, A., and Pateria, N.K., 1983, Acute encephalopathy in children in Nagpur: Similarity to Reye's syndrome. *Indian Journal of Pediatrics,* 50 : 129-132.

355. John, T.J., Mammen, K.C., Date, A., and Kamath, K.R., 1969, Acute encephalopathy and fatty degeneration of the viscera: A study of three cases in India. *Indian Journal of Medical Research,* 57 (12): 1865-1871.

356. Joseph, J., 1991, A study of the self concept of the handicapped. *Mind,* 17 (3): 1-6.

357. Joshi, H.D., Shah, T.B., and Damany, S.J., 1963, Gargoylism: A case report. *Indian Journal of Child Health,* 12 (8): 526-529.

358. Joshi, N.C., and Kittur, D., 1987, Neonatal neurobehavioural assessment and outcome. *Indian Pediatrics,* 24 (1): 69-76.

359. Joshi, P.L., Bhattacharrya, M., Rastogi, A.K., Divedi, S., Raj, B., and Varma, J., 1988, Handicapped persons: A demogRaohic profile in a rural area of Uttar Pradesh. *Disabilities and Impairments,* 2 (2): 135-141.

360. Joshi, R.N., Shah, M.J., Trivedi, N.B., and Joshi, H.D., 1986, Duchenne muscular dystrophy: Recent concepts. *Indian Journal of Pediatrics,* 53 (6): 775-780.

361. Joshi, V.S., and Shiroli, B., 1960, Inio-trichobezaor. *Indian Journal of Pediatrics,* 27 (151): 294-296.

362. Joshua, G.E., 1973, Hepatolenticular degeneration, Wilson's disease and rickets in children. *Indian Journal of Medical Research,* 61 (12): 1876-1884.

363. Joshua, G.E., 1974, Mental retardation in children: A aetiological study of 303 cases. *Indian Pediatrics,* 11 : 47-51.

364. Joshua, G.E., 1974, The genetic component in mentally retarded south Indian children. *Indian Journal of Medical Research,* 62 (8): 1251-1260.

365. Joshua, G.E., Basu, D.K., and Mathai, K.V., 1975, Sphingolipid errors in mental retardation in Indian children. *Indian Journal of Medical Research,* 63 (10): 1521-1528.

366. Joshua, G.E., Bhaktaviziam, A., Doss, S.T., and Basu, D.K., 1974, GM_2 gangliosidosis in a south Indian child: A clinico-pathological, biochemical study. *Indian Journal of Medical Research,* 62 (4): 788-799.

367. Joshua, G.E., John, E., and Jadhav, M., 1968, Phenylketonuria: The first in Andhra Pradesh. *Indian Pediatrics,* 5 : 382-385.

368. Joshua, G.E., Nair, N.G., and Radhakrishnan, A.N., 1973, Phenylketonuria in Tamil Nadu. *Indian Journal of Pediatrics,* 40: 245-252.

369. Jyothy, A., Uma, S.M., Reddy, P.P., Rani, P.U., and Pasricha, S., 1982, Diet theRaoy in phenylketonuria. *Indian Pediatrics,* 19 (9): 545-560.

370. Jyothy, A., and Reddy, P.P., 1984, Screening for aminoacid disorders in mental retardation. *Indian Pediatrics,* 21 p 381-388.

371. Jyothy, A., and Reddy, P.P., 1988, A centralised approach for amino acid disorder in the new born. *Disabilities and Impairments,* 2 (2): 131-134.

372. Jyotsna, M., 1985, Social worker in special schools. *The Indian Journal of Social Work,* 45 (4): 423-427.

373. Kagalwala, T.Y., Bharucha, B.A., Kumta, N.B., and Naik, G.G., 1988, Mucopolysaccharidoses: A study of 48 cases. *Indian Journal of Pediatrics,* 55 (6): 919-925.

374. Kakatkar, S., 1985, Parents campaign project. *The Journal of Rehabilitation in Asia,* 26 (2): 7-8.

375. Kalra, A., Bhatia, R., Kalra, K., Dayal, R.S., Dutt, T., Pandey, D.J., and Singh, Y.P., 1987, Ocular manifestations in mentally retarded children. *Indian Pediatrics,* 24 (5): 409-413.

376. Kalra, A., Misra, M.N., Kumar, R., Prasad, R., and Dayal, R.S., 1980, The impact of malnutrition on intelligence. *Indian Pediatrics,* 17 : 109-116.

377. Kalra, K., Singhal, K.C., and Bansal, O.P., 1965, Tay Sachs disease. *Indian Journal of Pediatrics,* 32 (212): 363-366.

378. Kalra, S.K., Sarakar, P., Vatwani, V., and Dey, N.C., 1983, A longitudinal study of low birth weight babies. *Indian Journal of Pediatrics,* 50 : 279-283.

379. Kandharkar, V.A., Patil, P.S., and Kirtane, S.S., 1979, Tuberous sclerosis. *Indian Journal of Pediatrics,* 46 (383): 445-450.

380. Kapadia, G.P., 1971, Rehabilitation of Handicapped. *The Nursing Journal of India,* 53 (10): 327.

381. Kapur, S., 1964, Helping the mentally retarded II : The role of a nurse in helping the mentally retarded. *The Nursing Journal of India,* 45 (9): 257-258.

382. Kapur, S., 1969, Evaluation of tuberculous meningitis since the use of steroid as an adjuvant. *Indian Pediatrics,* 6 : 166.

383. Kapur, S., Mammen, K.C., Jesudian, G., Mathew, K.C., and Kumar, G., 1972, Criteria to define prematurity in south India. *Indian Journal of Medical Research,* 60 (10): 1533-1542.

384. Kar, A.M., Mishra, V.K., Shukla, R., Nag, D., and Agarwal, S.K., 1980, Spina bifida and mirror movements. *Indian Pediatrics,* 17: 559-561.

385. Karunakaran, E.K., and Gupta, S., 1969, Agenesis of the corpus collosum: Report of a case. *Indian Journal of Pediatrics,* 36 (260): 325-327.

386. Karunanidhi, A., Rolston, R., John, L., Koshy, T.S., and Kanakasabapathy, A.S., 1982, Thyroid function in clinical euthyroid patients treated for hyperthyroidism. *Indian Journal of Medical Research,* 71, (11): 723-727.

387. Kaul, K.K., 1960, Serum ionogram in third degree malnutrition: Oedematous malnutrition. *Indian Journal of Pediatrics,* 27 (144): 1-8.

388. Kaul, K.K., 1960, Serum ionogram in third degree malnutrition: Marasmic malnutrition. *Indian Journal of Pediatrics,* 27 (144): 9-14.

389. Kaul, K.K., 1972, Syndrome of tremors in Indian infants. *Journal of Indian Medical Association,* 59 : 473.

390. Kaul, K.K., Belapurkar, K.M., and Parekh, P., 1972, The syndrome of tremors in infants: A long follow up. *Indian Journal of Medical Research,* 60 (7): 1067-1072.

391. Kaul, K.K., Dodeja, K., and Mehra, K.P., 1964, A true hermophrodite with some clinical features of Turner's syndrome. *Indian Pediatrics,* 1 (4): 156-60.

392. Kaul, K.K., Prasan, N., and Chowdhary, R.M., 1965, Some clinical observations and impressions on a syndrome of tremor's in infants from India. *Indian Journal of Pediatrics,* 32 : 1158-1166.

393. Kaul, K.K., Prasan, N., and Chowdhary, R.M., 1969, Further observations on the syndrome of tremors in infants. *Indian Pediatrics,* 6 : 219.

394. Kaul, K.K., Taluja, R.K., and Srivastava, A.K., 1970, Nutritional status of rural preschool children around Jabalpur: Anthropometric observation. *Indian Pediatrics,* 7 : 313.

395. Kaul, K.K., and Bhandari, N.R., 1959, Polydactylo-syndactylism in seven generations. *Indian Journal of Pediatrics,* 26 (132): 18-20.

396. Kaul, K.K., and Munjal, N., 1960, Waren Tay sachs disease. *Indian Journal of Child Health,* 9 (8): 440.

397. Kaur, R., 1977, Coping with mentally retarded. *Journal of Social Welfare,* 23 : 10.

398. Kaur, R., and Sen, A.K., 1974, Training and education of the mentally retarded children: A survey report. *Indian Journal of Mental Retardation,* 7 : 65-71.

399. Kaushik, S.S., 1984, Behaviour modification workshop for parents and teachers of mentally retarded: Programme evaluations. *The Journal of Rehabilitation in Asia,* 25 (2): 47.

400. Kaushik, S.S., 1987, Maintenance of treatment gains in retardate client care workers in institutionalised setting. *Disabilities and Impairments,* 1 (1&2): 21-30.

401. Kelkar, N., 1985, Vocational training for adolescent handicapped: An experiment. *The Journal of Rehabilitation in Asia,* 26 (1): 44-48.

402. Khandekar, M., 1974, A study of dropouts. *The Indian Journal of*

Social Work, 34 (4): 367-385.

403. Khandekar, M., and Joshi, P., 1973, Assessing nutritional status of preschool children: Some organisational considerations. *The Indian Journal of Social Work,* 34 (1): 11-25.

404. Khandelwal, M.K., 1958, Gargoylism: A case report. *Indian Journal of Child Health,* 7 (12): 713.

405. Khanna, K.K., and Prasad, L.S.N., 1967, Congenital malformations in the new born. *Indian Journal of Pediatrics,* 34 (230): 63.

406. Khanna, R., Sharma, L.N., and James, M.X., 1991, Tuberous sclerosis: Report on an unusual family. *Indian Journal of Psychiatry,* 33 (4): 314-317.

407. Khatua, S.P., 1961, Tuberculous meningitis in children. *Journal of Indian Medical Association,* 37 : 332.

408. Khatua, S.P., Manocha, B.K., Chatterjee, S., and Palodni, P.K.R., 1979, The incidence and aetiology of small for date infants born at term. *Indian Pediatrics,* 16 : 395-402.

409. Khatua, S.P., Saha, D., Khatua, S., and Pal, S.B., 1987, Early growth of term small for date infants in relation to caloric intake. *Indian Journal of Pediatrics,* 54 (5): 695-701.

410. Khetarpal, S.K., and Sarin, G.S., 1964, Gargoylism: A study of four cases. *Indian Journal of Pediatrics,* 31 (192): 21-23.

411. Khorana, A.B., 1969, Pyrithioxine, Encephabol, in the treatment of mental retardation. *Indian Journal of Mental Retardation,* 2 (2): 108-114.

412. Khosla, B.S., Malhotra, R., and Dutt, V., 1988, Sports as intervention for socialisation and integration of the mentally handicapped. *Indian Journal of Disability and Rehabilitation,* 2: 19-24.

413. Kishore, B., and Jain, C.K., 1969, Mental retardation: A proposed classification for use in India. *Indian Journal of Mental Retardation,* 2 (2): 80-86.

414. Kochhar, K.S., and Bharmota, H.S., 1965, Trichobezoar. *Journal of Indian Medical Association,* 45 : 361.

415. Kohli, A., and Verma, S.K., 1988, Mothers estimate of the intelligence of their mentally handicapped child. *Child Psychiatry Quarterly,* 21 (3): 129-136.

416. Kohli, T., 1981, Magnitude of disability problems and trends in intervention to prevent and rehabilitate the mentally retarded. *Indian Journal of Mental Retardation,* 14 (2): 79-90.

417. Kohli, T., 1982, Appraising innovative helping strategies for the education and training of mentally retarded. *Indian Journal of*

Mental Retardation, 15 (1): 10-18.

418. Kohli, T., 1989, Emerging trends in early intervention services for childhood disability. *Indian Journal of Disability and Rehabilitation,* 3 (1): 71-73.

419. Kohli, T., 1989, Trends and opinions: Emerging trends in early intervention services for childhood disability. *Indian Journal of Disability and Rehabilitation,* 3 (1): 71-74.

420. Kohli, T., 1990, Impact of home, centre based training programme in reducing developmental deficiencies of disadvantaged children. *Indian Journal of Disability and Rehabilitation,* 4 (2): 65-74.

421. Kowli, S.D., 1963, The placement of the handicapped in open employment. *The Indian Journal of Social Work,* 24 (3): 193-201.

422. Krishnamurthy, D.S., Patel, Z.M., and Khanna, S.A., 1981, Frequency of trisomy 21, translocation, mosaicism and familial cases of Down's syndrome in Bombay. *Indian Journal of Medical Research,* 73 : 218-222.

423. Krishnamurthy, D.S., Roy, S., Contractor, P.M., and Shah, V.C., 1984, Partial trisomy 21g,g21 qter, in a child with Down's syndrome. *Indian Journal of Pediatrics,* 51 : 363-366.

424. Krishnamurthy, K., and Malhotra, P., 1987, Identification and management of rural mentally handicapped children utilising health workers. *Child Psychiatry Quarterly,* 20 (1): 13-18.

425. Krishnamurthy, P.S., 1969, Homeopathy in mental retardation. *The Retarded,* 1 (1): 17-18.

426. Krishnaswamy, S., 1990, Role of handicapped in the aid of the handicapped. *The Indian Journal of Social Work,* 51 (1): 165-175.

427. Krupanidhi, I., Gowda, K.A., and Nirmala, N.S., 1964, The use of Nilamide in mental retardation in childhood. *Indian Journal of Pediatrics,* 31 (203): 351-354.

428. Kulkarni, R.D., Sadre, N.L., Bhide, N.K., and Aswin, R., 1958, Congenital galactosemia: Case report. *Indian Journal of Medical Research,* 46 (5): 938.

429. Kumar, N., Kumar, S., Parkash, A., and Varma, K.P.S., 1970, Trichobezoar: Report of a case. *Indian Journal of Pediatrics,* 37 (267): 160-162.

430. Kumar, S., Agarwal, A.K., Prasad, M., and Dutt, K., 1991, Mental retardation experiences in children attending anganwadis. *Mind,* 17 (3): 5-9.

431. Kumar, S., Jain, S., Sethi, G.R., Yadav, M., Saili, A., and Lal, U.B., 1988, A simple method of screening for intrauterine growth

retardation at birth. *Indian Journal of Pediatrics,* 55 (2): 283-286.

432. Kumar, S., and Kumar, N., 1972, Dermatoglyphic analysis as a diagnostic tool in Down syndrome. *Indian Journal of Pediatrics,* 39 (289): 39-47.

433. Kumaraswamy, R.N., Joshi, U.G., and Kulkarni, K.S., 1991, A profile of mentally retarded persons seen in Child Guidance Clinic of a teaching hospital. *Indian Journal of Clinical Psychology,* 18 (2): 45-48.

434. Kumari, P.S., 1981, Anaesthesiologist and the disabled patients. *The Journal of Rehabilitation in Asia,* 22 (4): 25-30.

435. Kumari, S., Ghosh, S., Bhargava, S.K., and Bhargava, V., 1972, Development of low birth weight babies. *Indian Pediatrics,* 9 : 732.

436. Kuppuswamy, B., 1968 A survey of mental retardation among children enrolled in middle schools of Mysore city. *Indian Journal of Mental Retardation,* 1 (1): 12-19.

437. Kurrien, J., 1979, Non formal education for rural dropouts: A critique of the Bhumiadhar model. *The Indian Journal of Social Work,* 39 (4): 409-424.

438. Kutar, M.J., 1948, Education of the mentally retarded. *The Indian Journal of Social Work,* 8 (4): 302-309.

439. Laha, P.N., Dev, A.M., and Misra, N.P., 1956, Tuberculous meningitis in infants and children. *Indian Journal of Pediatrics,* 23 (103): 313-316.

440. Lakshminarayana, L., 1990, Translocation Down's syndrome. *Indian Journal of Pediatrics,* 57 (2): 265-271.

441. Lal, H., 1965, Ellis van Crevaid syndrome. *Indian Journal of Pediatrics,* 32 : 10.

442. Lal, N., and Sethi, B.B., 1977 Estimate of mental ill health in children of urban community. *Indian Journal of Pediatrics,* 44 (350): 55-64.

443. Lal, R.S., 1973, Mentally retarded and discipline. *Social Welfare,* 19 : 5.

444. Lal, S.K., Surya, N.C., and Anantharamar, V., 1963, Galactosemia: An interesting case of survival. *Indian Journal of Medical Research,* 51 (1): 77.

445. Lalita, R., 1983, Helping the handicapped. *The Nursing Journal of India,* 66 (4): 90-92.

446. Lingam, S., 1992, Child Development: Pre-screening, screening and super screening. *Indian Journal of Pediatrics,* 59 : (c).

447. Madhavan, M., and Venkataramiah, N.R., 1970, Congenital

malformations: A clinicopathological study. *Indian Journal of Pediatrics,* 37 (267): 139-142.

448. Madhavan, T., Kalyan, M., and Menon, D.K., 1988, Development and evaluation of a training programme for rehabilitation workers in mental retardation: Report of field trial of training manuals. *Indian Journal of Disability and Rehabilitation,* 2 : 35-42.

449. Madhavan, T., Menon, D.K., Kumari, R.R.G.S., and Kalyan. M., 1990, Mental retardation awareness in the community. *Indian Journal of Disability and Rehabilitation,* 4 (1): 9-21.

450. Madhavan, T., and Narayan. J., 1988, Manual assymetries in persons with Down's syndrome. *Indian Journal of Psychiatry,* 30 (2): 193-196.

451. Madhavan, T., and Narayan. J., 1990, The role of consanguinity in the causation of mental retardation. *Indian Journal of Psychological Medicine,* 13 (1): 83-87.

452. Madhavan, T., and Narayan, J., 1990, A study of persons with severe mental retardation and multiple disabilities. *Indian Journal of Psychiatry,* 32 (4): 334-340.

453. Madhavan, T., and Narayan, J., 1992, Impact of intervention on the parental perceptions and expectations of their mentally retarded children. *The Indian Journal of Social Work,* 43 (2): 191-201.

454. Mahadevan, I., 1962, Social factors in some nutritional deficiency diseases. *The Indian Journal of Social Work,* 23 (1): 41-52.

455. Mahajan, C.M., Walia, B.N.S., and Dutta, B.N., 1971, Infantile tremor syndrome. *Indian Pediatrics,* 8 : 831.

456. Mahajan, C.M., Walia, B.N.S., and Parkash, A., 1971, Anaemias in infantile tremor syndrome. *Indian Journal of Pediatrics,* 38 (284): 362-364.

457. Mahapatra, G.B., 1966, Consanguinity: A review. *Indian Journal of Pediatrics,* 33 (224): 275-280.

458. Mahapatra, G.B., and Walia, B.N.S., 1964, The diagnosis of mentally subnormal child: A review. *Indian Pediatrics,* 1 (9): 365-368.

459. Majumdar, P.P., 1987, DNA markers and genetic diseases: Recent advances. *Bulletin of Human Genetics,* 12 (1): 9.

460. Malhotra, A.K., Saimbi, C.S., Chawla, T.N., and Rastogi, S., 1982, Comparative assessment of dental health in physically and mentally handicapped individuals. *Journal of Indian Dental Association,* 54 (10): 371-374.

461. Malhotra, H.K., Khanna, B.C., and Verma, S.K., 1973, Idiot savant: Review with a case report. *Indian Journal of Psychiatry,*

15 (5): 49-55.

462. Malhotra, K.K., Deo, M.G. Kapur, M.M., and Shah, P.K.D., 1969, Chromatin positive Klinefelter's syndrome. *Indian Journal of Medical Research,* 57 (3) 543-549.

463. Malhotra, R., and Agarwal, R., 1988, Change in adaptive behaviour of developmentally slow children: A longitudinal study. *Indian Journal of Disability and Rehabilitation,* 2 : 23-48.

464. Malhotra, S., 1990, Temperament characteristics of mentally retarded children. *Indian Journal of Pediatrics,* 57 (2): 213-218.

465. Malhotra, S., and Chadda, R., 1987, Specific developmental disorders in children attending a Child Guidance Clinic. *Indian Journal of Psychiatry,* 29 (4): 343-347.

466. Malik, G.K., Saksena, P.N., Rastogi, G.C., Shukla, R., and Wakhlu, I., 1979, Tay-Sachs disease. *Indian Journal of Pediatrics,* 46 (382): 425-426.

467. Malik, G.K., and Srivastava, R.K., 1979, A clinical study of Tuberculous meningitis in children from rehabilitative point of view. *The Journal of Rehabilitation in Asia,* 20 (1): 9-12.

468. Malin, A.J., 1968, Adaptation of Wechslers Intelligence Scale for Indian Children. *The Journal of Rehabilitation in Asia,* 9 : 19-20.

469. Malin, A.J., 1968, Psychological tests for retarded Indian children. *The Journal of Rehabilitation in Asia,* 9 : 1.

470. Malin, A.J., 1969, Comparing WISC scores of American and Indian mentally retarded children. *Indian Journal of Mental Retardation,* 2 (1): 27-30.

471. Malin, A.J., 1971, Malins intellingence scale for Indian children. *Indian Journal of Mental Retardation,* 4 (1&2): 15-20.

472. Malin, A.J., 1971, Guidance and mentally retarded. *Journal of Vocational and Educational Guidance,* 14 (1): 23-27.

473. Malin, A.J., 1972, Training programmes for the teachers of the mentally retarded. *The Journal of Rehabilitation in Asia,* 13 (2): 9-12.

474. Malin, A.J., 1973, Landmarks "down under" in mental retardation. *Indian Journal of Mental Retardation,* 6 (1): 21-23.

475. Malin, A.J., 1973, Hopes for the retarded in Asia. *Indian Journal of Mental Retardation,* 6 (2): 51-54.

476. Malin, A.J., 1974, Report of the first Pan Asian conference on mental retardation at Manila. *The Journal of Rehabilitation in Asia,* 15 (4): 17-18.

477. Mallya, I.P., 1979, Special play sessions: A play method to help children with special needs. *Child Psychiatry Quarterly.* 12 (1):

1-6.

478. Malvia, S.N., 1973, Parents of the mentally retarded. *Social Welfare,* 19 : 7.

479. Manchanda, K.S., Paul, G., and Narang, A., 1979, The Laurence Moon Bardet Biedl syndrome with renal involvement. *Indian Journal of Pediatrics,* 46 (383): 460-462.

480. Manchanda, S.S., 1958, Mental deficiency in children: A review of 220 cases. *Indian Journal of Child Health,* 7.

481. Manchanda, S.S., 1960, Gargoylism: Report of four cases with brief review. *Indian Journal of Pediatrics,* 27 (151): 281.

482. Manchanda, S.S., 1961, Anencephaly: A case report. *Indian Journal of Child Health,* 10 3, 143.

483. Manchanda, S.S., and Amritsar, H.L., 1966, Tuberculous meningitis in children: A problem unsolved in India. *Indian Pediatrics,* 3 (5): 167-176.

484. Manchanda, S.S., and Culera, J.S., 1958, Mongolism in children: A review of 35 cases. *Indian Journal of Child Health,* 7 : 101.

485. Manchanda, S.S., and Gupta, H.C., 1954, Acute epidemic of encephalitis in children at Amritsar: An analysis of 45 cases. *Indian Journal of Child Health,* 3 : 341.

486. Manchanda, S.S., and Lal, S.K., 1956, Congenital galactosemia. *Indian Journal of Child Health,* 5 (12): 611-612.

487. Manchanda, S.S., and Lal, S.K., 1966, Tuberculous meningitis in children: A problem unsolved in India. *Indian Pediatrics,* 3 (4): 167.

488. Manchanda, S.S., and Sharma, R.N., 1958, Hypothyroidism in children: Analysis of 12 cases and a brief review. *Indian Journal of Pediatrics,* 25 (119): 1-10.

489. Manchanda. S.S., and Singh, H., 1960, Tuberculous meningitis in children: An analysis of 90 cases with special emphasis on some factors influencing the prognosis. *Indian Journal of Pediatrics,* 27 (144): 26-33.

490. Mandal, J., and Mitra, T.P., 1988, A comparative study of amino acid disorders among mentally retarded children. *Disabilities and Impairments,* 2 (1): 1-8.

491. Mane, P.N., 1990, Coping with the developmentally delayed child: The trials and tribulations of parents. *The Indian Journal of Social Work,* 51 (1): 553-565.

492. Marfatia, J.C., 1952, Mentally handicapped children. *The Indian Journal of Social Work,* 13 (2): 81-88.

493. Marfatia, J.C., 1953, Use of thyroid in retarded speech development.

The Indian Journal of Social Work, 14 (2): 185-191.

494. Marfatia, J.C., 1968, The social and emotional problems of the mentally handicapped: Some hints to parents. *Child Psychiatry Quarterly,* 1 (4): 1-5.

495. Marwah, V., and Shamimuddin, M.K., 1972, Some aspects of rehabilitation problems of the handicapped. *The Journal of Rehabilitation in Asia,* 13 (1): 12-13.

496. Master, R.S., 1981, Tuberous sclerosis: A case study. *Child Psychiatry Quarterly,* 14 (3): 72-78.

497. Master, R.S., 1984, Mental retardation: A review. *Child Psychiatry Quarterly,* 17 (1&2): 41-64.

498. Master, R.S., 1984, Multidisciplinary rehabilitation of the mentally retarded. *Indian Journal of Psychiatry,* 26 (1): 88-92.

499. Mathew, A., 1986, Social work practice in schools for the mentally retarded. *Child Psychiatry Quarterly,* 19 (1): 45-48.

500. Mathur, G.P., Dayal, R.S., Prasad, R., and Mathur, S., 1969, Tremors, mental and physical retardation, light colored haired and anemia in malnourished children. *Indian Pediatrics,* 6, : 483-494.

501. Mathur, G.P., Prasad, R., and Dayal, R.S., 1961, Gargoylism. *Indian Journal of Pediatrics,* 28, : 381.

502. Mathur, G.P., and Kushwaha, K.P., 1986, Superstitions in pediatric practice. *Indian Pediatrics,* 23 : 159-161.

503. Mathur, P.S., 1957, Gargoylism. *Indian Journal of Pediatrics,* 24 (118): 372-374.

504. Mathur, P.S., and Srivastava, S.P., 1958, Amarautic familial idiocy. *Journal of Indian Medical Association,* 31 : 25.

505. Mathur, S., 1976, Scholastic backwardness. *Indian Journal of Mental Retardation,* 9 : 3[illegible]-34.

506. Mathur, S., 1985, Socio-economic profile of handicap population in Parel village, Bombay. *The Journal of Rehabilitation in Asia,* 25 (1): 1-10.

507. Mathur, S., and Nalwa, V., 1986, Misconceptions about mental retardation. *Journal of Personality and Clinical Studies,* 2 (1): 57-60.

508. Mathur, S., and Nalwa, V., 1987, Misconceptions about mental retardation. *Indian Journal of Clinical Psychology,* 14 (1): 19-21.

509. Mazumdar, B.N., Prabhu, G.G., and Neki, J.S., 1971, Special education and environment. *Indian Journal of Mental Retardation,* 5 (1): 25-32.

510. Mazumdar, B.N., and Prabhu, G.G., 1972, Role of parents in the management and education of the retarded. *Indian Journal of Mental Retardation,* 5 : 13-18.

511. Mazumdar, B.N., and Prabhu, G.G., 1972, Mental retardation: Parents perception of the problem. *Child Psychiatry Quarterly,* 5: 13-16.

512. Mazumdar, L., 1977, Making the mentally retarded independent. *Swasth Hind,* 21 : 360.

513. Mc Connel, T.S., 1981, Helping the disabled: An integrated approach. *Mental Health Review,* 1 (1): 9-13.

514. Mehrotra, K.K., 1974, Vocational evaluator. *The Journal of Rehabilitation in Asia,* 15 (1): 27-29.

515. Mehta, G., Venkatachalam, P.S., and Gopalan, C., 1956, Steatorrhoea in nutritional oedema syndrome,Kwashiorkor, *Indian Journal of Medical Research,* 44 (4): 727.

516. Mehta, H.P., 1978, The use of psychological tests with the mentally retarded. *Indian Journal of Mental Retardation,* 11 (1): 11-22.

517. Mehta, I.B., 1979, Working for scouting and guiding for handicapped children. *The Journal of Rehabilitation in Asia,* 20 (3): 24.

518. Mehta, J.B., 1962, Morbidity and mortality in children: Handicapped children. *Indian Journal of Child Health,* 11 (6): 258-261.

519. Mehta, M., Bhargava, M., and Pande, P., 1990, A proposed model for the behaviour training of mentally handicapped children through parent participation. *Indian Journal of Disability and Rehabilitation,* 4 (1): 1-8.

520. Mehta, M., and Ochaney, M., 1984, Mental Retardates: Involving mothers in operant conditioning programme. *Indian Journal of Clinical Psychology,* 11 (2): 45-49.

521. Mehta, M.M., Chablani, U.A., Contractor, N.M., Bhatia, H.M., Sighal, B.S., Mondkar, V.P., and Desai, A.D., 1986, HLA- A and HLA-B antigens in multiple sclerosis, motor neurone discase and Duchenne muscular dystrophy. *Indian Journal of Medical Research,* 75 (5): 519-521.

522. Mehta, N.R., 1961 Tuberculous meningitis. *Journal of Indian Medical Association,* 37 : 10.

523. Mehta, S., Teja, J.S., Wig, N.N., Thukral, S., and Pasricha, S., 1975, Protein calorie malnutrition: A follow up study. *Indian Journal of Medical Research,* 63 : 576.

524. Menon, B., 1979, The disabled are part of society. *Social Welfare,* 26 (4): 53.

525. Menon, D.K., 1988, Human resource development in mental

retardation: Editorial. *Indian Journal of Disability and Rehabilitation,* 2 : 2.

526. Menon, D.K., Vijayalakshmi, M., and Madhavan, T., 1987, A review of training manuals on mental handicap. *Indian Journal of Disability and Rehabilitation,* 1 : 13-22.

527. Menon, P.S.N., Sachdev, H.P.S., Verma, I.C., and Ghai, O.P., 1981, Developmental milestones: Downs syndrome patients in north India. *Indian Journal of Medical Research,* 73 : 369.

528. Menon, S.N., 1987, Facilities for the handicapped,Editorial, *Indian Journal of Disability and Rehabilitation,* 1 : 1-5.

529. Menon, S.N., 1987, Schemes and facilities for the handicapped, Editorial, *Indian Journal of Disability and Rehabilitation,* 2:1-6.

530. Merchant, R.H., 1985, Birth asphyxia: Predictors of outcome and management. *Indian Journal of Pediatrics,* 52 (419): 609-614.

531. Merchant, S.M., 1956, Tuberculous meningitis: Report of 23 cases treated with ACTH or cortisone. *Indian Journal of Child Health,* 5 (1): 45.

532. Merchant, S.M., and Thandani, I.P., 1972, Clinical and obstetric features of low birth weight babies. *Indian Pediatrics,* 9 : 127.

533. Miles, M., 1980, Counselling parents of a retarded child. *The Journal of Rehabilitation in Asia,* 21 (2): 32-37.

534. Milne, J., and Matthew, P., 1980, Advisors to disabled: Job analysis. *The Journal of Rehabilitation in Asia,* 21 (4): 22-26.

535. Mishra, L.S., 1986, A clinical study of course and effect of alcoholism and drug addiction by parents of mentally retarded children. *Child Psychiatry Quarterly,* 19 (2&3): 117-121.

536. Mishra, L.S., Saxena, N.K., and Pathak, M.P., 1981, Some psycho-economic factors associated with mental retardation. *Indian Journal of Mental Retardation,* 14 (2): 41-46.

537. Mishra, L.S., Saxena, N.K. and Pathak, M.P., 1982, Psychoclinical symptoms and factors associated with natal history of mentally retarded children. *Child Psychiatry Quarterly,* 15 (4): 119-123.

538. Misra, M.N., Kalra, K., and Dayal, R.S., 1976, Analysis of mentally retarded cases attending the Child Guidance Clinic. *Indian Journal of Pediatrics,* 43 (339): 88-95.

539. Misra, P.K., Tandon, P.N., and Bajpai, P.C., 1971, Infantile tremor syndrome: Probable aetiology. *Indian Pediatrics,* 8:62-64.

540. Misra, P.K., and Kaul, R., 1980, PhototheRaoy in neonatal hyperbilirubinemia. *Indian Journal of Pediatrics,* 47 (385): 109-115.

541. Misra, R.P., 1958, Management of marasmus. *Indian Journal of*

Pediatrics, 25 (129): 566-572.

542. Mital, V.K., and Grewal, R.S., 1969, Congenital anomalies in neonates. *Indian Journal of Pediatrics,* 36 (261): 356-365.

543. Mitra, S.C., 1968, Human anencephalic monsters. *Indian Journal of Pediatrics,* 35 (249): 480-483.

544. Mitra, S.C., and Venkataraman, G., 1973, Endocrine glands in Anencephaly. *Indian Journal of Pediatrics,* 40 : 197.

545. Mitra, S.S., 1977, Seven cases of G6 PD deficiency. *Indian Journal of Medical Research,* 65 (2): 253-258.

546. Mittal, R.N., Singh, N., and Nand, S., 1967, Trichobezoar. *Indian Journal of Pediatrics,* 34 (233): 206-209.

547. Mittal, S.K., 1969, Cerebellar disorders in childhood: A review. *Indian Journal of Pediatrics,* 36 (259): 294-300.

548. Mixon, J.C., and Dev, V.G., 1986, Fragile x syndrome: Clinical, cytogenetic, biochemical and molecular features. *Indian Journal of Pediatrics,* 53 (4): 451-459.

549. Mody, J., 1985, Social worker in special schools. *The Indian Journal of Social Work,* 45 (4): 421.

550. Mohan, B., 1969, Social policy for the welfare of the mentally retarded: A plea for reorientation. *Indian Journal of Mental Retardation,* 2 (1): 7-13.

551. Mohan, B., 1971, On planning social security for the mentally retarded in India. *Indian Journal of Mental Retardation,* 4 (1&2): 26-33.

552. Mohan, B., 1971, Social security for the mentally retarded. *Social Welfare,* 17 : 13.

553. Mohan, D., 1988, Socio technical correlates of disability and projections for future trends in India. *Indian Journal of Disability and Rehabilitation,* 2 : 49-62.

554. Mohan, J., 1972, Mental retardation, giftedness and physical persistance. *Indian Journal of Mental Retardation,* 5 (1&2): 33-39.

555. Mohan, J., 1977, Problems of research and social work in mental retardation. *Indian Journal of Mental Retardation,* 10 (2): 88-93.

556. Mohan, J., 1989, Reaction time, psychomotor performance, vigilance and fluctuation of attention of mentally retarded, normal and gifted children. *Disabilities and Impairments,* 3 (1): 57-62.

557. Mohan, J., Bhandari, A., and Sehgal, M., 1982, A study of personality and adjustment problems of mentally retarded children. *Indian Journal of Mental Retardation,* 15 (1): 38-42.

558. Mohan, J., Sehgal, M., and Bhandari, A., 1982, Training and

education of mentally retarded: Some theoretical and psychological considerations. *Indian Journal of Mental Retardation,* 15(1):1-9.

559. Mohan, J., and Menon, D.K., 1968, Mental retardation and physical persistence. *Indian Journal of Mental Retardation,* 1, (2): 63-66.

560. Mohan, J., and Menon, D.K., 1969, Extraversion, neuroticism, feeble mindedness and physical persistence. *Indian Journal of Mental Retardation,* 2 (1): 31-33.

561. Mohan, V., and Rai, N., 1976, Nature of task and its effect on recall of interrupted tasks in mentally retarded children. *Indian Journal of Mental Retardation,* 9 ( ): 35-44.

562. Mohan, V., and Sethi, L., 1968, A study of personality of mentally deficient children. *Indian Journal of Mental Retardation,* 1 (2): 67-74.

563. Mohan, V., and Suri, U., 1972, A comparative study of the effect of personality on performance of the normal and mentally retarded children. *Indian Journal of Mental Retardation,* 5 (1): 18-24.

564. Mohanty, A., and Goel, S.K., 1990, Relationship of reading comprehension with metalinguistic skills in children. *Indian Journal of Disability and Rehabilitation,* 4 (2): 95-102.

565. Moorthy, M.V., 1943, Rehabilitation of the Indian war disabled. *The Indian Journal of Social Work,* 4 (3): 241-255.

566. Moudgil, A.C., 1970, Teaching menstrual hygeine to a mentally retarded. *Indian Journal of Mental Retardation,* 3, (1): 50-54.

567. Moudgil, A.C., Kumar, H. and Sharma, S., 1985 Buffering effect of social, emotional support on the parents of mentally retarded children. *Indian Journal of Clinical Psychology,* 12 (2): 63-67.

568. Moudgil, A.C., Kumar, H. and Sharma, S., 1985, Hospitalisation facilities for mentally retarded children. *Indian Journal of Clinical Psychology,* 12 (2): 79-84.

569. Mudgil, A., Singh, S.B., and Srivastava, J.R., 1982, An aetiological and psychological study of mentally retarded children. *Indian Pediatrics,* 19 (8) : 689-693.

570. Mujoo H.N., Shukla, S.K., and Gupta, T.P., 1969, Literature on mental retardation: I. *Indian Journal of Mental Retardation,* 2 (1): 39-62.

571. Mujoo H.N., and Shukla S.K., 1970, Evaluation of the terms 'mental retardation' and 'mentally retarded people' by a sample of university students. *Indian Journal of Mental Retardation,* 3 (1): 60-68.

572. Mukherjee, D.K., and Sethana, N.J.C., 1970, Birth weight and its relation with certain maternal factors. *Indian Journal of Pediatrics,* 37 : 460.

573. Mukherjee, K.L., 1965, The mechanism of fatty liver in Kwashiorkor: A review. *Indian Pediatrics,* 2 (3): 76-84.

574. Mukherjee, S., and Mukherjee, S.N., 1971, A study of premature births. *Indian Journal of Pediatrics,* 38 (285): 389-392.

575. Mukopadhya, B., 1980, Disability preventive services in India. *The Journal of Rehabilitation in Asia,* 21 (1): 16-25.

576. Mundkur, N., Singh, M.V., and Gupta, S., 1979, Impact of socio-economic status of the development of small for dates between 3-4 years. *Indian Pediatrics,* 16 (11): 979-984.

577. Munjal, N., and Thakar, S.V., 1964, Trichobezoar: A case report. *Indian Pediatrics,* 1 (11): 455-460.

578. Murari, P., and Sinha, V., 1978, A study on place of origin of institutionalised mentally deficient children. *Psycho-Lingua,* 8 (1): 31-33.

579. Murthy, D.S., Krishna, S.K., Murthy, J.K., Patel, and Tyagi, A.F., 1989, Nucleolar organiser region hetromorphism associated with trisomy 21: A risk factor for non disjunction?. *Indian Journal of Experimental Biology,* 27 (4): 864-867.

580. Murthy, D.S.K., Prajapati, B.S., and Desai, A.B., 1984, Down's syndrome associated with absent patella: A case report. *Indian Journal of Pediatrics,* 51 p 729.

581. Murthy, D.S.K., Roy, S., Contractor, P.M., and Shah, V.C., 1984, Trisomy 21q: 46 XX s+/47 xx+ 2pq-(q22q+cr), (mosaicism,de novo) in the Down's syndrome child. *Indian Journal of Pediatrics,* 51 : 363.

582. Murthy, H.N., 1966, Problems of borderline children. *Experiments in Secondary Education,* 11 (3): 18-20.

583. Murthy, H.V.V., 1991, Birth weight and the associated factors: A review. *The Indian Journal of Social Work,* 52 (2): 251-256.

584. Murthy, R.S., 1974, Mental retardation: Scope for prevention: I Nutrition. *Indian Journal of Mental Retardation,* 7 (2): 49-57.

585. Murthy, R.S., 1981, Training village level workers for the identification and care of the mentally handicapped children. *Mental Retardation Newsletter,* 7 : 19-21.

586. Murthy, R.S., Wig, N.N., Manchanda, M., and Dhir, A.M., 1981, Community care of the mentally handicapped in the rural areas. *Social Welfare,* 28 : 4.

587. Murthy, R.S., Wig, N.N., and Dhir, A., 1980, Rural community

attitudes to mental retardation. *Child Psychiatry Quarterly,* 13 : 81-88.

588. Murthy, R.S., and Ghosh, A., 1973, Classification of mental retardation: An evaluation. *Indian Journal of Mental Retardation,* 6 (2): 67-74.

589. Murthy, S.K., Murthy, D.S.K., Shah, V.C., and Desai, A.B., 1987, Down syndrome in Ahmedabad: Karyotype analysis of sixty cases. *Indian Journal of Pediatrics,* 54 : 723-727.

590. Myreddi, V., 1992, Present trends in mental handicap in India. *Disabilities and Impairments,* 4 (1&2): 5-14.

591. Nagaraja, J., 1983, Mental Retardation, Editorial, *Child Psychiatry Quarterly,* 16 (3): i-ii.

592. Nagaraj, M.N., Shivashankar, N., and Narayanan, H.S., 1981, Efficacy of speech and language therapy with severe mentally retarded children. *Indian Journal of Psychological Medicine,* 4 (2): 93-97.

593. Nagpal, A., and Sen, A., 1981, Form discrimination learning in adolescent retardates. *University Psychology Research Journal,* 2 : 24.

594. Naidu, S., and Kalyan, M., 1992, Relationship between socially adaptive behaviours in Down's syndrome and controls. *Indian Journal of Clinical Psychology,* 19 (1): 10-13.

595. Nair, G.R., 1981, Welfare of the handicapped: The role of voluntary organistions. *Indian Journal of Public Administration,* 27 (3): 673.

596. Nair, K.P.B., and Rao B.S.S.R., 1971, Hartnups Disease. *Indian Journal of Pediatrics,* 38 (284): 375-377.

597. Nair, N.S., and Kunnakutti, N.K., 1965, Turner's syndrome: Report of a case. *Indian Pediatrics,* 2 (8): 307-309.

598. Nair, N.S., and Mathai, N.M.A., 1964, Congenital malformations in the newborn at Calicut. *Antiseptic,* 61 : 323.

599. Nair, N.S., and Nayar, T.C.V., 1965, D_1 trisomy syndrome. *Indian Journal of Pediatrics,* 32 (209): 194-196.

600. Nalwa, V., and Mathur, S., 1984, Personality concommitants of educable mentally retarded children in three different institutions. *Indian Journal of Clinical Psychology,* 11 (2): 111-117.

601. Nanda, J.L., 1970, A challenge of mental retardation: Problems of mentally retarded children. *Social Welfare,* 17 : 4.

602. Nanda, S., 1977, What is mental retardation? *Swasth Hind,* 21 : 351.

603. Nanda, S., 1978, Some probable factors causing mental retardation. *Child Psychiatry Quarterly,* 11 (4): 106-111.

604. Nandi, D.N., Ajmany, S., Ganguly, H., Banerjee, G., Boral, G.C., Ghosh, A., and Sarkar, S., 1975, Psychiatric disorders in a rural community in West Bengal: An epidemiological study. *Indian Journal of Psychiatry,* 17 : 87.

605. Nandi, D.N., Ajmany, S., Ganguly, H., Banerjee, G., Boral, G.C., Ghosh, A., and Sarkar, S., 1976, The incidence of mental disorders in one year in a rural community in West Bengal. *Indian Journal of Psychiatry,* 18 : 78.

606. Nandi, D.N., Das, N.N., Chaudhuri, A., Banerjee, G., Datta, P., Ghosh, A., and Boral, G.C., 1980, Mental morbidity and urban life: An eidemiological study. *Indian Journal of Psychiatry,* 22 : 324.

607. Narayan, J., 1989, Functional programming for the mentally retarded persons. *Indian Journal of Disability and Rehabilitation,* 3 (1): 47-50.

608. Narayan, J., Madhavan, T., and Mukhopadhyaya, S., 1990, A study of children with poor scholastic performance. *Indian Journal of Psychological Medicine,* 13 (2): 173-186.

609. Narayan, J., Rao T.A.S., and Stephenson, L.A., 1990, Effect of orientation of rural health workers on their level of awareness on mental retardation. *Disabilities and Impairments,* 4 (1): 10-18.

610. Narayan, J., and Ajit, M., 1991, Development of skills in a mentally retarded child: The effect of home training. *Indian Educational Review,* 26 (3): 29-41.

611. Narayan, S., 1992, Community based rehabilitation for the mentally handicapped: A model. *The Indian Journal of Social Work,* 51 (1): 157-164.

612. Narayana, V., and George, V.C., 1970, Conditionability of mental defectives. *Transactions of All Indian Institute of Mental Health,* 10 : 71.

613. Narayanan, H.S., 1978, Parental consanguinity and mental retardation. *Medical Genetics in India,* 2 : 141-144.

614. Narayanan, H.S., Gandhi, D.S., and Girimaji, S.R., 1988, Prader Labhard Willi syndrome: A report of 23 cases. *NIMHANS Journal,* 6 (1): 19-21.

615. Narayanan, H.S., Girimaji, S.R., Gandhi, D.S., Maruthiraju, K., Rao, P.M., and Nardev, G., 1988, Brief inpatient family intervention in mental retardation. *Indian Journal of Psychiatry,* 30 (3): 275-281.

616 Narayanan, H.S., Mohan, K.S., Jayasimha, N., and Rao, B.S.S.R., 1987, Some paradoxical observations noted in the prevalence of Hurler's and Hunter's syndrome. *Indian Journal of Psychiatry,* 29 (2): 169-171.

617. Narayanan, H.S., Mohan, K.S., Jayasimha, N., and Rao, B.S.S.R., 1987, Hyperphosphatasea neurologic deficits and mental retardation in four siblings. *Indian Journal of Psychiatry,* 29 (3): 291-292.

618. Narayanan, H.S., Mohan, K.S., Jayasimha, N., and Rao, B.S.S.R., 1987, A clinical and biochemical study of the mucopolysacchridosis. *Indian Journal of Pediatrics,* 54 (2): 123-126.

619. Narayanan, H.S., Mohan, K.S., and Rao, B.S.S.R., 1986, Detection of mental retardation at early stages by parents and its management. *Indian Journal of Psychological Medicine,* 9 (1): 33-37.

620. Narayanan, H.S., Rao, B.S.S.R., Rao, P.M., and Subbukrishna, D.K., 1986, A study of 361 cases of severe unclassified mental retardation with recurrence in the families. *Indian Journal of Psychiatry,* 28 (4): 277-280.

621. Narayanan, H.S., Rao, B.S.S.R., Rao, P.M., and Subbukrishna, D.K., 1988, Clinical and genetic studies in cases of phenylketonuria and a report of follow up after dietary theRaoy. *Indian Journal of Psychiatry,* 30 (2): 123-127.

622. Narayanan, H.S., Rao, B.S.S.R., and Manjunath, K.R., 1986, Cytogenetic and dermatoglyphic patterns of Down's syndrome cases. *NIMHANS Journal,* 4 (2): 91-104.

623. Narayanan, H.S., Rao, B.S.S.R., and Reddy, G.N.N., 1973, A clinical survey of 1200 cases of mental retardation with a brief report on some very rare types. *Indian Journal of Psychiatry,* 15 (2): 143-146.

624. Narayanan, H.S., Rao, P.M., Subbukrishna, D.K., and Rao, B.S.S.R., 1987, Observation of mentally retarded cases with special reference to consanguinity. *NIMHANS Journal,* 5 (2): 121-123.

625. Narayanan, H.S., Reddy, G.N.N., and Rao, B.S.S.R., 1970, Some observations made during a multidisciplinary approach in investigating cases seen at the Mental Retardation Clinic, Part One: DemogRaohic and clinical aspects. *Transactions of All India Institute for Mental Health,* 10 : 59.

626. Narayanan, H.S., Reddy, G.N.N., and Rao, B.S.S.R., 1973, Multiple affected sib ships with mental retardation. *Indian Journal of Psychiatry,* 15 (4): 378-381.

627. Narayanan, H.S., Subhash, M.N., and Rao, B.S.S.R., 1974,

Neuropsychiatric disorders and lipidoses. *Kerala Journal of Psychiatry,* 2 (1): 11-15.

628. Narayanan, H.S., and Girimaji, S.R., 1986, Parental self help group movement in mental retardation. *Community Mental Health News,* 3&4 : 9-10.

629. Narayanan, H.S., and Rao, B.S.S.R., 1978, Psychoses associated with homocystinuria: A case report. *Indian Journal of Psychiatry,* 20 : 98-100.

630. Narayanan, I., Gupta, A., Mandal, R.N., Chugh, R.K., and Singh, S., 1987, Infant feeding and early neonatal jaundice. *Indian Journal of Pediatrics,* 54 (2): 257-260.

631. Natarajan, M., 1983, Disability detection and evaluation for social assistance. *The Journal of Rehabilitation in Asia,* 24 (2): 23-33.

632. Nazareth, F.A., and Patel, M.P., 1956, Trichobezoar. *Indian Journal of Child Health,* 5 (6): 361.

633. Neki, J.S., and Manchanda, S.S., 1964, Reflections on epiloia: A report of five cases. *Indian Pediatrics,* 1 (4): 136-145.

634. Nikam, M., 1981, Movement education and theRaoy for adolescent developmentally handicapped. *Mental Health Review,* 1 (2): 45-54.

635. Nimbkar, K.V., 1974, Living with your disabilities or where there is a will there is a way. *The Journal of Rehabilitation in Asia,* 15 (3): 53.

636. Nityagopal, A., 1983, The causes and consequences of protien energy malnutrition. *Social Welfare,* 30 (1): 16.

637. Nizamie, A., Nizamie, S.H., James, M.X., and Shukla, T.R., 1989, Assessment of mental retardation: Need for newer approaches. *Indian Journal of Psychiatry,* 31 (4): 305-310.

638. Ojha, A.B., 1977, The myth of non-deprivation. *Indian Journal of Mental Retardation,* 10 (1): 25-41.

639. Ojha, K.N., 1975, Psychological assessment of mentally retarded children. *Indian Journal of Clinical Psychology,* 2 (2): 45-50.

640. Ojha, K.N., 1981, International Year of Disabled Persons, (IYDP): A challenge to clinical psychologists. *Indian Journal of Clinical Psychology,* 8 (2): 77-79.

641. Ojha, K.N., 1992, Rehabilitation of persons with handicaps: Community participation, Guest Editorial, *Disabilities and Impairments,* 4 5 (1&2): 1-4.

642. Ojha, K.N., Verma, S.K., and Sinha, A.K., 1976, Psychological evaluation of change and progress in the mentally retarded: Implications for teachers and parents. *The Journal of Rehabilitation*

in Asia, 17 : 1-6.

643. Ojha, K.N., Verma, S.K., and Sinha, D., 1976, Psychological evaluation of change and progress in the mentally retarded. *The Journal of Rehabilitation in Asia,* 17 (3): 27-32.

644. Oza, D.K., 1976, Attitudes of the handicapped trainees: A case study. *The Journal of Rehabilitation in Asia,* 17 (4): 4-6.

645. Oza, G.C., Shah, P.M., and Parikh, M.M., 1963, Marfans syndrome. *Indian Journal of Child Health,* 12 (12): 815-818.

646. Paddaiah, G., and Reddy, G.G., 1980, Effect of consanguinity on anthropometric measurements in the newborn. *Indian Journal of Pediatrics,* 47 (385): 133-136.

647. Pai, G.B., 1977, Plea for a comprehensive legislation for the mentally retarded. *Mental Retardation Digest,* 6 : 7.

648. Pai, G.S., 1986, Genetic counselling in pediatric practice. *Indian Journal of Pediatrics,* 53 (4): 471-476.

649. Pai, R.A., 1967, Cytogenic anomalies in children. *Indian Pediatrics,* 4 (3): 145.

650. Pai, V.A., 1977, Mental retardation: A global view with emphasis on India. *Swasth Hind,* 21 : 346.

651. Pamela, H.S., 1980, Music: A milieu factor with implications for nurse theRaoist. *Journal of Psychiatric Nursing,* 18 (6): 28-33.

652. Panda, K.C., 1974, A process approach for research into retardate parental family: Theoretical and methodological considerations. *Indian Journal of Mental Retardation,* 7 (1): 14-24.

653. Panda, K.C., and Goel, S.K., 1987, The mentally retarded in mainstream: Concept, issues and policy. *Disabilities and Impairments,* 1 (1&2): 41-53.

654. Panda, K.C., and Lynch, W.W., 1973, Relationships among scores on intellectual achievement, responsibility and cognitive style measures in educable mentally retarded children. *Indian Journal of Mental Retardation,* 6 (2): 55-66.

655. Panda, K.C., and Lynch, W.W., 1974, Effects of race and sex on attribution of intellectual achievement responsibility for success and failure situations among educable mentally retarded children. *Indian Journal of Mental Retardation,* 7 (2): 72-80.

656. Pandav, C.S., and Kochupillai, N., 1982, Endemic goitre in India: Prevalence, aetiology, attendent disabilities and control measures. *Indian Journal of Pediatrics,* 50 : 259.

657. Pandav, C.S., and Kochupillai, N., 1985, Organisation and implementation of neonatal hypothyroid screening programme in India: A primary health care approach. *Indian Journal of Pediatrics,*

52 : 223-229.

658. Pandit, A., and Bhave, S., 1981, Prevalence and patterns of handicapped in rural areas. *Indian Pediatrics,* 18 (1): 35-39.

659. Pandit, M., Vijayalakshmi, G., Naik, U.S., and Plumber, G.R., 1988 Early intervention with infants at risk: A pilot study. *Child Psychiatry Quarterly,* 21 (1): 1-6.

660. Parande, A.S., 1967, Two cases of Niemann-Pick disease. *Indian Pediatrics,* 4.

661. Parekh, U.C., Udani, P.M., Naik, P.A., and Shah, B.P., 1974, Mental development of children with severe protein caloric malnutrition in the past and present. *Indian Pediatrics,* 11 : 465-469.

662. Parikh, A.P., 1990, Mental performance in Down's syndrome. *Indian Journal of Pediatrics,* 57 (2): 261-263.

663. Parikh, A.P., and Goyal, N.A., 1990, Epidemiology of Down's syndrome: A study of 395 cases. *Disabilities and Impairments,* 4 (1&2): 52-61.

664. Parikh, J., and Shukla, S., 1984, Mental health through integration for children with special needs. *Journal of Psychological Researches,* 28 (2): 77-83.

665. Parikh, J., and Yadav, R., 1979, Developing and evaluating a programme for the parents of developmentally handicapped children. *Indian Journal of Mental Retardation,* 12 (1&2): 63-70.

666. Parikh, J.B., and Shukla, S., 1982, Mental health through "integration" for children with special needs. *Journal of Psychological Researches,* 1 (1): 77-83.

667. Parikh, J.K., 1981, An experiment with helping parents of developmentally handicapped children. *Child Psychiatry Quarterly,* 14 (3): 79-84.

668. Parikh, J.K., 1988, Infant stimulation programmes for mentally handicapped children and parental involvement. *Disabilities and Impairments,* 2 (1&2): 81-88.

669. Pasricha, S., Verma, S.K., Mehta, S., and Wig, N.N., 1972, Relationship of parental education and IQ with IQ of malnourished children: A study in nature-nurture relationship. *Indian Journal of Mental Retardation,* 5 (1&2): 58-63.

670. Patel, Y.P., 1985, The impact of study habits of intellectually backward pupils upon their academic achievement. *Indian Psychological Review,* 28 (3): 7-13.

671. Pathak, A.K., and Sharma, N.L., 1968, Syndrome of retarded growth obesity, muscular hypotonia and mental deficiency, Prader

Willi syndrome, *Indian Journal of Pediatrics,* 35 : 447.

672. Pathak, M.P., Saxena, N.K., and Mishra, L.S., 1983, Some psychological factors associated with mental retardation. *Child Psychiatry Quarterly,* 16 (3): 116-122.

673. Pathak, M.P., and Mishra, L.S., 1985, A study of relationship between milestone development and neurotic traits among mentally retarded. *Indian Psychological Review,* 28 (2): 5-9.

674. Pathak, M.P., and Mishra, L.S., 1986, Relationship between milestone development and neurotic traits among mentally retarded. *Indian Journal of Clinical Psychology,* 13 (1): 5-8.

675. Pathak, P., 1969, Baroda longitudinal study: Mental and motor growth of Indian babies from 1 month to 30 months. *Indian Pediatrics,* 6 : 147.

676. Pathak, P., 1973, Application of Bayley scales of infant development to neurological cases. *Indian Pediatrics,* 10 : 147.

677. Pattarkine, A.G., 1971, Sheltered workshop for the mentally retarded. *Social Welfare,* 17 : 15.

678. Paul, S.S., 1963, Pyogenic meningitis in children. *Indian Journal of Child Health,* 12 (2): 98.

679. Paul, S.S., Gupta, S., and Mohindra, S., 1954, Cerebrospinal fluid otorrhoea in a case of purulent meningitis. *Indian Journal of Child Health,* 3 (10): 509-512.

680. Paurikh, J., and Dhylon, R., 1988, Integrating handicapped children in the regular class: An evaluation. *Disabilities and Impairments,* 2 (1): 53-58.

681. Pereira, S.M., Isaac, T., Begum, A., Dumm, M.F., and Webb, J.K.G., 1965, Moderate protein high calorie diets in treatment of kwashiorkor. *Indian Pediatrics,* 2 (3): 76-84.

682. Pershad, D., Kaushal, P., and Verma, S.K., 1973, Nueroticism scores of mothers of mentally retarded and of neurotic children. *Indian Journal of Mental Retardation,* 6 (1): 24-27.

683. Pershad, D., and Verma, S.K., 1980, Education and psychological test scores. *Indian Journal of Psychiatry,* 22 : 179-181.

684. Pershad, D., Verma, S.K., and Randhawa, A., 1979, A preliminary report on a performance test of intelligence on 4-8 years old children. *Indian Journal of Educational Psychology,* 6 (1) 125-130.

685. Peshawaria. R., 1989, Parent involvement in the training and management of their mentally handicapped persons. *Journal of Personality and Clinical Studies,* 5 (2): 217-221.

686. Peshawaria, R., Reddi, V.S., Subba Rao, T.A., Persha, A.J., and

Mohapatra, B., 1991, Group training programmes at NIMH: An overview. *Journal of Personality and Clinical Studies,* 7 (2): 169-174.

687. Peshawaria, R., Venkatesan, S., Mohapatra, B., and Menon, D.K., 1990, Teachers perceptions of problem behaviours among mentally handicapped persons in special school settings. *Indian Journal of Disability and Rehabilitation,* 4 (1): 23-30.

688. Peshawaria, R., Venkatesan, S., and Menon, D.K., 1988, Consumer demand of services by parents of mentally handicapped individuals. *Indian Journal of Disability and Rehabilitation,* 2 : 43-57.

689. Peshawaria, R., Venkatesan, S., and Menon, D.K., 1990, Behaviour problems in mentally handicapped persons: An analysis of parent needs. *Indian Journal of Clinical Psychology,* 17 (2): 63-70.

690. Peshawaria, R., and Menon, D.K., 1991, Needs of the families of mentally handicapped children. *Indian Journal of Disability and Rehabilitation,* 5 (1): 69-72.

691. Phadke, A., 1983, Sex chromosomal aberrations and their mode of presentation. *Indian Journal of Pediatrics,* 50 : 142-145.

692. Phatak, P., Barve, S., and Pajnigar, F., 1988, Motor and mental development of high risk babies during first two years of life. *Psychological Studies,* 33 (3): 194-199.

693. Pohowala, J.N., 1956, Serous phase of purulent meningitis simulating tuberculous meningitis. *Indian Journal of Pediatrics,* 23 (106): 415-420.

694. Pohowala, J.N., Kaul, K.K., Bhandari, N.R., and Singh, S.D., 1960, Infantile meningo-encephalitic syndrome. *Indian Journal of Pediatrics,* 27 (145): 49-54.

695. Prabhu, G.G., 1968, The participation of the parents in the services for the retarded. *Indian Journal of Mental Retardation,* 1 (1): 4-11.

696. Prabhu, G.G., 1968, Speech problems of the mentally retarded. *Indian Journal of Mental Retardation,* 1 (2): 87-94.

697. Prabhu, G.G., 1969, Professional training in India in the sphere of mental retardation. *Indian Journal of Mental Retardation,* 2 (2): 98-107.

698. Prabhu, G.G., 1970, A study of parents needs for institutional facilities for the retarded. *Indian Journal of Mental Retardation,* 3 (1): 21-24.

699. Prabhu, G.G., 1970, Personality characteristics of parents who over estimate the potentialities of their retarded child. *Indian Journal of Mental Retardation,* 3 (1): 55-61.

700. Prabhu, G.G., 1977, Clinical and domiciliary management of a mentally retarded child. *Swasth Hind,* 21 : 356.

701. Prabhu, G.G., and Raguram, A., 1984, Measurement of intelligence and its usefulness. *Indian Journal of Pediatrics,* 51 (409): 225-234.

702. Praharaj, K.C., Mohanta, K.D., Nanda, C.N., and Pana, G.K., 1969, Encephalitis in children: A clinical study. *Indian Journal of Pediatrics,* 36 (253): 25-29.

703. Prakash, O., and Sen, A.K., 1986, Sociological correlates of intelligence in rural children. *Social Change,* 16 (1): 27-33.

704. Prasad, L., 1961, Vocational rehabilitation of the disabled in Asia. *The Indian Journal of Social Work,* 22 (2): 121-128.

705. Prasad, L.S.N., 1953, Report of case of gargoylism. *Indian Journal of Pediatrics,* 20 : 172.

706. Prasad, L.S.N., Singh, K.P., and Rahman, M., 1965, Observation on EEG changes in progressive muscular dystrophy. *Indian Pediatrics,* 2 (9): 321-329.

707. Prasad, M., Dwivedi, C.M., Kumar, S., and Rastogi, S.N., 1988, Mental subnormality and social class. *Journal of Personality and Clinical Studies,* 4 (2): 183-186.

708. Prasad, M., Sitholey, P., Dutt, K., and Srivastava, R.P., 1992, Activities of daily living, training and treatment of temper tantrums in a severely retarded aphasic child. *Indian Journal of Clinical Psychology,* 19 (1): 37-39.

709. Prasad, M., and Prasad, D., 1973, A comparative study of short term memory span. *Indian Journal of Mental Retardation,* 6 (2): 102-107.

710. Prasad, M., and Sitholey, P., 1988, Behaviour theRaoy in a retarded adolescent with conduct disorder: A case report. *Indian Journal of Clinical Psychology,* 15 (2): 74-76.

711. Prasad, S., 1958, Gargoylism. *Indian Journal of Child Health,* 7 (6): 343.

712. Prasad, S., 1962, Observations on clinical manifestations of tuberculous meningitis in children. *Indian Journal of Pediatrics,* 29 (170): 69-74.

713. Prasad, T.V.H., 1988, Early development, rehabilitation and social integration. *Indian Journal of Disability and Rehabilitation,* 2 : 63-78.

714. Prasan, N.G., Mukherjee, J.P., and Kaul, K.K., 1965, Tremors in infancy. *Indian Pediatrics* 2 (7): 252-256.

715. Prathnidhi, A.K., Shrotri, A.N., Shah, V., and Bodani, M.D.,

1956, Domiciliary care of low birth weight neonates. *Indian Journal of Pediatrics,* 53 (1): 87-92.

716. Prema, T.P., Devarajaiah, C., Reddamma, K., and Gopinath, P.S., 1987, Recreational activities for the mentally retarded. *The Nursing Journal of India,* 68 (8): 207-209.

717. Puri, R.K., Khanna, K.K., Bhargava, I., and Balakrishna, S., 1979, Role of consanguinity in chromosomal syndromes. *Indian Journal of Medical Research,* 68 (4): 859-864.

718. Purohit, K.R., and Bhai, Y.D., 1967, A case of galactosemia. *Indian Pediatrics,* 4 (12): 454-55.

719. Purohit, N.N., Purohit, M., and Garg, O.P., 1977, Apert's syndrome. *Indian Journal of Pediatrics,* 44 (356): 284-286.

720. Radhakrishnan, S., 1979, Curriculum training schedules for mentally handicapped. *Mental Retardation Digest,* 7 : 26.

721. Rahman, H., Agarwal, V.K., and Srivastava, A.K., 1979, Spina bifida and cranium bifidium. *Indian Journal of Pediatrics,* 46 (377): 210-214.

722. Rai, G.C., 1988, A study of discrimination, generalisation and difference limen of mentally retarded. *Journal of Personality and Clinical Studies,* 4 (1): 11-15.

723. Rai, K., 1989, Behaviour of mentally retarded children: The effect of environment. *Journal of Indian Education,* 14 (5): 22-30.

724. Rai, K., 1993, Management of the mentally retarded in family environment. *Journal of Indian Education,* 17 (6): 24-32.

725. Rajalakshmi, R., 1979, Malnutrition in children: Its pattern and prevention. *The Indian Journal of Social Work,* 40 (3): 283-293.

726. Rajaram, S., Parthasarathy, R., and Shariff, I.A., 1987, Social experiments in community living for mentally disabled: Evolution of psychiatric social work model in community setting. *The Journal of Rehabilitation in Asia,* 28 (1): 1-4.

727. Ram, S.P., and Pal, N.L., 1964, Cerebromuscular degeneration. *Indian Pediatrics,* 1 : 487.

728. Ram, V., and Palsane, M.N., 1979, Diagnosis of mental retardation: Combining the measures of intelligence and social maturity. *Indian Journal of Mental Retardation,* 12 (1&2): 18-23.

729. Ramachandran, R.S., 1963, Some observations of 733 premature babies admitted in premature unit of the women and children hospital, Egmore, Madras. *Indian Journal of Child Health,* 12 (5): 279.

730. Ramachandran, R.S., Ramanathan, K., and Indra, G., 1970, Tuberculous meningitis: A review of 288 cases in children. *Indian*

Journal of Pediatrics, 37 (266): 85-88.

731. Ramakrishnan, K., Mathew, K.N., and Thomas, K., 1982, Causes of fever in febrile seizures. *Indian Journal of Pediatrics,* 49 p 367.

732. Ramakrishnan, K., and Thomas, K., 1986, Long term prophylaxis of febrile seizures. *Indian Journal of Pediatrics,* 53 (3): 397-400.

733. Ramakumar, L., and Goyal, B.G., 1966, An unusual form of gigantism. *Indian Journal of Pediatrics,* 33 (222): 205-207.

734. Ramakumar, L., and Pancove, S.P., 1975, Infantile Tremor syndrome. *Indian Journal of Pediatrics,* 42 (331): 215-225.

735. Ramalingaswamy, V., 1981 Rehabilitation for the disabled: Policy and organisational issues. *Indian Journal of Public Administration,* 27 (3): 546-548.

736. Ramalingaswamy, V., 1984. Community based rehabilitation of the disabled: Challenge and opportunity. *The Journal of Rehabilitation in Asia,* 25 ( ): 70-73.

737. Raman, T.S.R., and Verma, C.M., 1990, Obstructive hydrocephalus. *Indian Pediatrics,* 27 (10): 1106-1108.

738. Ramanathan, M.K., 1955, Biochemical changes in the serum in nutritional oedema syndrome, Kwashiorkor, *Indian Journal of Medical Research,* 43 (3): 517-520.

739. Ramanathan, M.K., Venkatachalam, P.S., Srikantia, S.G., and Gopalan, S., 1955, A follow up study of 100 cases of nutritional oedema syndrome, Kwashiorkor, *Indian Journal of Medical Research,* 43 (2): 285.

740. Ramanujam, B.K., 1968, Paediatrics, child development and mental retardation. *Indian Journal of Mental Retardation,* 1 (1): 38-47.

741. Ramanujam, B.K., and David, S., 1969, A clinical study of 100 cases of mentally retarded children seen in a clinic for the mentally retarded. *Indian Pediatrics,* 6 (2): 118.

742. Ramchandran, R.S., 1963, Some observations on premature babies. *Indian Journal of Child Health,* 12 (5): 279-288.

743. Ramdas, G., and Mishra, R.R., 1987, Rural attitudes towards the disabled. *Indian Journal of Disability and Rehabilitation,* 1 : 49-53.

744. Ranganathan, M., and Parthasarthy, R., 1984, Vocational rehabilitation of mentally disabled persons: An Indian perspective. *The Journal of Rehabilitation in Asia,* 25, (2): 39-46.

745. Rani, A.S., and Reddy, P.P., 1990, Screening of mentally retarded children for Fragile X syndrome. *Disabilities and Impairments,* 4 (1): 40-44.

746. Rani, S., Seth, S., and Seth, P.K., 1979, Serum proteins in the mentally retarded. *Indian Journal of Mental Retardation,* 12 (1&2): 24-30.

747. Rao, A.M., 1967, Cerebromascular degeneration: Late infantile form. *Indian Journal of Pediatrics,* 34 (228): 13-16.

748. Rao B.S.N., 1979, Three cases of homocystinuria. *Journal of Association of Physicians,* 27 : 28-42.

749. Rao, B.S.N., and Gopalan, C., 1957, Some aspects of hair changes in kwashiorkor. *Indian Journal of Medical Research,* 45 (1): 85-93.

750. Rao, B.S.S.R., 1965, Cerebro-spinal fluid changes in central nervous system disorders. *Indian Journal of Medical Research,* 53 (11): 1078-1083.

751. Rao, B.S.S.R., Jayasimha, N., and Subhash, M.N., 1981, Biochemical screening in mental retardation. *Indian Journal of Pediatrics.* 48 : 229-234.

752. Rao, B.S.S.R., Jayasimha, N., and Subhash, M.N., 1982, Biochemical screening and mental retardation. *Indian Journal of Pediatrics,* 49 : 361-365.

753. Rao, B.S.S.R., Narayanan, H.S., and Reddy, G.N.N., 1970, Hartnup's disease. *Indian Pediatrics,* 7 : 637.

754. Rao, B.S.S.R., Subhash, M.N., and Narayanan, H.S., 1977, Metabolic anomalies detected among mentally retarded children. *Indian Journal of Mental Retardation,* 10 (2): 24-31.

755. Rao, B.S.S.R., and Chandrakala, B.I.L., 1983, Inborn errors of metabolism : A review of cases of IEM reported from India. *NIMHANS Journal,* 9 (1): 1-8.

756. Rao, B.S.S.R., and Narayanan, H.S., 1976, Consanguinity and familial mental retardation. *Journal of Medical Genetics,* 13 (1): 27-29.

757. Rao, B.S.S.R., and Narayanan, H.S., 1977, Metabolic anomalies detected during a systematic biochemical screening of mentally retarded cases. *Indian Journal of Medical Research,* 65 (2): 241-247.

758. Rao, D.L.N.M., 1963, Mental deficiency. Transactions of All *India Institute for Mental Health,* 3 : 1.

759. Rao, G.P., 1988, Late and delayed problems of Down's syndrome patients. *Indian Journal of Pediatrics,* 55 (3): 353-355.

760. Rao, G.V.N., 1981, Dental treatment requirement of socially and mentally handicapped children of Mysore State. *The Journal of Rehabilitation in Asia,* 22 (1): 17-20.

761. Rao, K., Barnabas, I.P., and Gopinath, P.S., 1989, Behaviour modification in rehabilitation setting. *Journal of Personality and Clinical Studies,* 5 (1): 23-27.

762. Rao, K.S., Satyanarayana, M., and Sarvalakshmi, D., 1973, A study of Down's syndrome in coastal Andhra Pradesh. *Indian Pediatrics,* 10 : 671-673.

763. Rao, K.S., Savithri, C., Murthy, N.V.R., and Satyanarayana, M., 1974 D_1 trisomy syndrome: Report of a case. *Indian Journal of Pediatrics,* 41 312, 22.

764. Rao, M.N., 1990, Integrating the disabled : A reality?. *The Indian Journal of Social Work,* 5 (1): 149-156.

765. Rao, P.H., Venkatesan, S., and Vepuri, V.G.D., 1994, Employment opportunities for mentally handicapped individuals in rural areas: A proposed model. *Journal of Indian Academy of Applied Psychology,* ppo.

766. Rao, P.G., 1977, Self employment schemes. *The Journal of Rehabilitation in Asia,* 18 (3): 30.

767. Rao, P.R., 1979, Thirty four cases of G6 PD deficiency. *Indian Journal of Medical Research,* 68 : 807-813.

768. Rao, P.S.S.S., Inbaraj, S.G., and Kaliaperumal, V.G., 1971, An epidemiological study of consanguinity in a large south Indian town. *Indian Journal of Medical Research,* 59 (2): 294-301.

769. Rao, P.S.S.S., and Inbaraj, S.G., 1978, A prospective study of infant mortality and congenital malformations in relation to intrauterine growth rates in south India. *Indian Journal of Medical Research,* 67, (2): 245-254.

770. Rao, P.T., Chitra, D.R., and Krishnaiah, H.G., 1959, A study of the early clinical science and biochemical values of cerebro spinal fluids in the course of tuberculous meningitis during treatment and other factors influencing the prognosis. *Indian Journal of Pediatrics,* 26 (136): 178-186.

771. Rao, P.T., Khan, A.M., and Anjaiah, K., 1972, Comparative trial of Liv 52 and Orabolin in marasmus. *Indian Journal of Pediatrics,* 39 (294): 227-230.

772. Rao, P.V., 1990, Childhood disability in Andhra Pradesh. *Social Change,* 20 (3): 53-57.

773. Rao, S.B., and Dinkar, I., 1970, Intracranial tumors in children. *Indian Journal of Pediatrics,* 37 (275): 501-503.

774. Rao, S.B., and Dinkar, I., 1970, Spinal tumors in children. *Indian Journal of Pediatrics,* 37 (264): 4-6.

775. Rao, T.A.S., and Srinivas, N.C., 1990, Speech and language

deficits and mental retardation: A report on the analysis of 300 mentally retarded persons. *Indian Journal of Disability and Rehabilitation,* 3 (2): 31-43.

776. Rao, T.V., Mushtaq, S., Das, S., and Shankar, S.K., 1986, Multiple sclerosis with associated diffuse Oligodendroglioma. *NIMHANS Journal,* 4 (2): 105-110.

777. Rao, V., 1982, Services for the handicapped persons: Organisational and policy implications. *The Indian Journal of Social Work,* 43 (4): 351-368.

778. Rao, W.G.R., 1978, The disabled, too on warpath. *The Journal of Rehabilitation in Asia,* 19 (1): 24-25.

779. Rao, W.G.R., 1979, Indian Society for the Rehabilitation of the Handicapped, Bombay. *The Journal of Rehabilitation in Asia,* 20 (3): 38-39.

780. Rastogi, C.K., 1981, Attitude of parents towards their mentally retarded children. *Indian Journal of Psychiatry,* 23 (3): 206-209.

781. Rastogi, C.K., 1984, Personality pattern of parents of mentally retarded children. *Indian Journal of Psychiatry,* 26 (1): 46-50.

782. Ratnaswami, L., Mammen, K.C., and John, T.J., 1978, Encephalopathy and fatty degeneration of the viscera: A study of seven cases. *Indian Pediatrics,* 15 (4): 174-179.

783. Ravar, J.M., and Vankar, G.K., 1992, Parental involvement in care, training and management of mentally handicapped. *Mind,* 18 (3): 33-41.

784. Reddy, K.S., Thomas, I.M., and Narayanan, H.S., 1986, Partial deletion of the long arm of chromosome 11: The Jacobsen syndrome. *Indian Journal of Pediatrics,* 53 (1): 123-126.

785. Reddy, K.S., and Thomas, I.M., 1985, Cytogenetic investigations in mentally retarded children. *Indian Journal of Medical Research,* 74 (8): 164-170.

786. Reddy, M.A., 1974, Screening for inborn errors of amino acid metabolism. *Indian Journal of Pediatrics,* 41 (315): 131.

787. Reddy, M.D.R., Karan, S., and Reddy, S.V., 1985, Neonatal gram negative pyogenic meningitis: TheRaoeutic evaluation. *Indian Journal of Pediatrics,* 52 (414): 53-56.

788. Reddy, S., Ramamurthy, P.V., and Reddy, R., 1991, A comparative study of sources of stress among disabled boys and girls. *Journal of Personality and Clinical Studies,* 7 (2): 125-130.

789. Reddy, S.N., 1987, Social work intervention in the rehabilitation of the mentally retarded. *Journal of Medical and Psychiatric Social Work,* 1 (1): 26-36.

790. Reddy, S.N., 1992, Community based rehabilitation: An experiment. *Disabilities and Impairments,* 4 (1&2): 28-37.

791. Reddy, V., 1972, Absorption of fat in kwashiorkor. *Indian Journal of Medical Research,* 60 (4): 628-631.

792. Reddy, V., Reddy, Y.R., Rao, B.S.N., and Sivakumar, B., 1972, A case of Maple Syrup Urine disease from Hyderabad. *Indian Pediatrics,* 9 : 629.

793. Reddy, Y.R., Rao, V.S., and Kumari, C.K., 1976, Dermatoglyphics in mental retardation. *Indian Pediatrics,* 13 (8): 629-633.

794. Rohtagi, S., 1981, Welfare of the disabled in India. *Yojana,* 25 (14&15): 8.

795. Rohtagi, S., 1981, Services of the disabled: Role of Central Social Welfare Board,CSWB, *Yojana,* 25 (4): 50.

796. Roy, I., Seth, P.K., and Seth, S., 1979, Trisomy 18 in mental retardation. *Indian Journal of Mental Retardation,* 12 (1&2): 6-11.

797. Roy, P.K., 1955, Description of a monstrosity. *Indian Journal of Pediatrics,* 22 (94): 247-248.

798. Sachdeva, K.K., Manchanda, S.S., and Lal, H., 1965, The syndrome of tremors, mental regression and anemia in infants and young children: A study of 102 cases. *Indian Pediatrics,* 2 (7): 239-251.

799. Saha, G.B., 1982, Some social aspects of mentally handicapped. *Samiksha,* 36 (1): 13-17.

800. Saha, R., Hotoj, M.K., Poddar, S.K., and Dey, A.K., 1992, Technical and employment opportunities for disabled in industry. *Indian Journal of Disability and Rehabilitation,* 6 (1): 51-60.

801. Sahasrabudhe, B.G., and Sancheti, K.H., 1980, Survey of handicapped. *The Journal of Rehabilitation in Asia,* 21 (4): 30-34.

802. Saifullah, S., Chandra, R.K., Pathak, I.C., and Dhall, G.I., 1967, Congenital malformations in newborn: A perspective longitudinal study. *Indian Pediatrics,* 4 (6): 251-261.

803. Saigal, S., 1986, The outcome of very low birth weight infants: Past, present and future. *Indian Journal of Pediatrics,* 53 (3): 365-371.

804. Saigal, S., and Srivastava, S.R., 1968, Newer clinical criteria for prematurity. *Indian Pediatrics,* 5 : 369.

805. Saili, A., Sarna, M.S., Haldar, D., Kumari, S., and Dutta, A.K., 1990, Delayed ceaserian section: Neonatal outcome. *Indian Pediatrics,* 27 (6): 601-604.

806. Sainata, M.K., Indira, O.C., and Mathai, N.M., 1972, Low birth weight babies. *Indian Journal of Pediatrics,* 39 (299): 389-396.

807. Saksena, P.N., Bajpai, P.C., and Dube, S.K., 1966, A clinical study of mongolism in Indian children. *Indian Journal of Pediatrics,* 33 (224): 281-287.

808. Saksena, P.N., Bajpai, P.C., and Dube, S.K., 1966, Evaluation of dermatoglyphics in mongolism. *Indian Journal of Pediatrics,* 33 (224): 298-306.

809. Saksena, P.N., Kumar, N., and Kumar, S., 1969, Evaluation of dermatoglyphics in Klinefelter's syndrome. *Indian Journal of Pediatrics,* 36 : 13.

810. Saksena, T.N., and Mathur, P.P., 1972, Evaluation of dermatoglyphics in mental deficiency. *Indian Pediatrics,* 9 (10): 627-628.

811. Samadhi, A., 1966, A comparison of certain aspects of kwashiorkor with those of normal children from the same community. *Indian Pediatrics,* 3 (4): 153-156.

812. Samadhi, A., 1967, Kwashiorkor in Kabul and Hyderabad. *Indian Pediatrics,* 4 (8): 300-334.

813. Sampat, M.B., and Sirsat, M.V., 1972, The thyroid gland in hyperthyroidism. *Indian Journal of Medical Research,* 60 (6): 851-858.

814. Santhanakrishnan, B.R., 1971, Rubinstein Taybis syndrome: Case reports. *Indian Journal of Pediatrics,* 38 (281): 276-278.

815. Sarkar, J., 1975, Comparative study of hostility between mentally retarded and subnormal children. *Indian Journal of Mental Retardation,* 8 : 1.

816. Sarma, M.K.J., and Rao P.S., 1982, Gangliosides in different regions of brain of small for date infants. *Indian Journal of Medical Research,* 71 (6): 816-819.

817. Satapathy, R.K., 1974, Survey of handicapped children in Behrampur town and its suburbs with special reference to their problems. *Indian Pediatrics,* 11 : 297-300.

818. Satyavathi, K., 1970, Educating the mentally retarded children. *Swasth Hind,* 14 : 324.

819. Saxena, K.M., and Pynles, C.V., 1965, Thyroid function in mongolism. *Indian Journal of Pediatrics,* 32 : 367.

820. Saxena, O., Saxena, S., and Ojah, D.G., 1967, Tuberous sclerosis. *Indian Pediatrics,* 4 (7): 281-299.

821. Saxena, S., Garg, D.P., and Saxena, O., 1966, Arthrogryposes multiplex congenita with mental deficiency: A case report. *Indian*

Pediatrics, 3 (5): 192-193.

822. Saxena, S., Sharma, J., and Saxena, O., 1968, Acrocephosyndactyly, Apert's syndrome,: Report of a case. *Indian Journal of Pediatrics,* 35 (249): 487-489.

823. Seethamma, H.N., and Majumdar, R.K., 1979, New rehabilitation law requires a clearer definition of handicap. *Rehabilitation Literature,* 40 (11&12): 340-341.

824. Sehgal, S., and Srivastava, J.K., 1969, Anthropometric studies of 1000 consecutive newborns with special reference to determine the criteria for prematurity. *Indian Journal of Pediatrics,* 36 : 24.

825. Sen, A., 1966, Effect of meaningful auditory distraction on a sorting task in imbeciles. *Bulletin of Council for Social and Psychological Research,* 7 (1) 1-8.

826. Sen, A., 1975, The concept of mental retardation. *Indian Journal of Mental Retardation,* 8 : 25-32.

827. Sen, A., 1976, Facets of deprivation and mental deficiency. *Indian Journal of Mental Retardation,* 9 (1&2): 62-70.

828. Sen, A., 1978 Mental retardation and crime. *Indian Journal of Mental Retardation,* 11 (2): 75-92.

829. Sen, A., 1978, Factors affecting transfer in the retarded. *Indian Journal of Mental Retardation,* 11 (1): 36-47.

830. Sen, A., 1979, Scope of prevention of mental retardation in India. *Social Change,* 9 (1&2): 35-42.

831. Sen, A., 1981, Education and care of the mentally retarded. *Indian Journal of Applied Psychology,* 18 (3): 700-712.

832. Sen, A., and Sen, A.K., 1967 A short introduction to the researches in the field of mental deficiency in England. *Bulletin of Council for Social and Psychological Research,* 8 (1): 20-25.

833. Sen, A., and Sen, A.K., 1968, The effect of distraction on a perceptual task in the subnormal. *Bulletin of Council for Social and Psychological Research,* 9 (2): 60-63.

834. Sen, A., and Sen, A.K., 1971, The effect of distraction on non verbal tasks in the subnormal: A series of experiments. *Indian Journal of Psychology,* 46 : 135-147.

835. Sen, A.K., 1966, The effect of stimulus length and display time in short term memory among imbeciles. *Bulletin of Council for Social and Psychological Research,* 7 (1): 12-19.

836. Sen, A.K., 1975, Mental retardation in India: An overview. *Indian Journal of Mental Retardation,* 8 : 1.

837. Sen, A.K., 1976, Some aspects of mental retardation. *Indian Journal of Mental Retardation,* 9 (1&2): 51-56.

838. Sen, A.K., 1982, Care, prevention and assessment of mental retardation in India. *The Journal of Rehabilitation in Asia,* 23 (3): 26-34.

839. Sen, A.K., and Patnaik, R., 1973, An experimental study of transfer of training in mental retardates. *Indian Journal of Psychology,* 48 : 11-20.

840. Sen, A.K., and Sen, A., 1969, The relationship between the memory and intelligence among mental retardates. *Indian Journal of Mental Retardation,* 2 (1): 1-5.

841. Sen, A.K., and Sen, A., 1969, Associative transfer as a function of prior learning in paired associate task among mentally defective. *Psychological Studies,* 14 (1): 60-63.

842. Sen, A.K., and Sen, A., 1969, Relationship between list length and free recall: Association or arousal. *Indian Journal of Experimental Psychology,* 3 (1): 16-19.

843. Sequiera, E., Lalitha, K., Hariharan, K., and Krishnaswamy, P.R., 1967, Metabolism of phenylalanime in clinical protein calorie malnutrition. *Indian Pediatrics,* 4 (1): 1-10.

844. Sequiera, E.M., Rao, P.M., Subbukrishna, D.K., and Prabhu,. G.G., 1990, Perceived burden and coping styles of the mothers of mentally handicapped. *NIMHANS Journal,* 8 (1): 63-67.

845. Sheshadri, M., Varma, V.K., Verma, S.K., and Pershad, D., 1983, Impact of a mentally handicapped child on the family. *Indian Journal of Clinical Psychology,* 10 (2): 473-478.

846. Seth, P., 1985, Rubella virus pregnancy and fetus,Annotations, *Indian Journal of Pediatrics,* 52 (417): 386-387.

847. Sethi, A.S., Verma, I.C., Mittal, S.K., and Khanna, K.K., 1968, Idiopathic hypoparathyroidism. *Indian Journal of Pediatrics,* 35 (249): 490-495.

848. Sethi, A.S., and Singh, M., 1969, Intrauterine growth and development. *Indian Journal of Pediatrics,* 36 (254): 82-90.

849. Sethi, B.B., 1979, Nutrition and mental retardation,Editorial, *Indian Journal of Psychiatry,* 21 (2): 97-99.

850. Sethi, B.B., 1980, 1981: Year of the Handicapped. *Indian Journal of Psychiatry,* 22 : 127.

851. Sethi, B.B., Gupta, S.C., Kumar, R., and Promilla, A., 1972, A psychiatric survey of 500 rural families. *Indian Journal of Psychiatry,* 14 : 183.

852. Sethi, B.B., Sharma, M., and Gupta, A.K., 1985, Community attitudes towards mental disorders. *Indian Journal of Social*

Psychiatry, 1 (1): 54-65.

853. Sethi, B.B., and Gupta, S.C., 1977, Two million people in Uttar Pradesh mentally retarded. *The Journal of Rehabilitation in Asia,* 18 (4): 38-39.

854. Sethi, B.B., and Sitholey, P., 1986, A study of time utilisation, perception of burden and help expectations of mothers of urban mentally retarded children. *Indian Journal of Social Psychiatry,* 2 (1&2): 25-44.

855. Sethna, K.J., 1978, Psychological problems created by mental retardation. *Community Psychiatry Journal,* 4 (1): 13-16.

856. Shah, A.V., Goswami, U.A. Maniar, R.C., Hajariwala, D.C., and Sinha, B.K., 1980, Prevalence of pscyhiatric disorders in Ahmedabad: An epidemiological study. *Indian Journal of Psychiatry,* 22 : 384.

857. Shah, A.V., and Hajariwala, D.C., 1978, Mental retardation and the general practitioner. *Doctor to Doctor,* 2 (4): 151-153.

858. Shah, D.K., Verma, S.K., and Teja, J.S., 1970, Differential problems in primary and secondary retardates. *Indian Journal of Mental Retardation,* 3 (1): 25-38.

859. Shah, G., 1989, Working with parents of handicapped children. *The Indian Journal of Social Work,* 50 (4): 483-495.

860. Shah, P.M., 1965, Observations of galactosemic families. *Indian Journal of Pediatrics,* 32 (215): 379-394.

861. Shah, P.M., Udani, P.M., and Aphale, R.V., 1971, Domiciliary management of kwashiorkor in rural setup: A longitudinal study of clinical, economical and social aspects. *Indian Pediatrics,* 8 : 805.

862. Shah. P.M., and Mahurkar, S.D., 1964, Galactosemia: Report of two cases. *Indian Pediatrics,* 1 (2): 58-64.

863. Shah, V.C, Krishnamurthy, D.S., and Murthy, S.K., 1990, Cytogenetic studies in a population suspected to have chromosomal abnormalities. *Indian Journal of Pediatrics,* 57 (2): 235-243.

864. Shambuji., 1982, Mental retardation: Its relation to malnutrition. *Indian Journal of Mental Retardation,* 15 (1): 30-34.

865. Shamim, F., 1979, Curriculum/training for mentally handicapped. *Mental Retardation Digest* 7 : 22.

866. Shankar, V., 1976, Emotional problems of the handicapped. *Asian Journal of Psychology and Education,* 1 (1): 39.

867. Shanti, I., Chaudhury, N.N.R., and Chandra, P.K., 1976, Small for date babies. *Journal of Indian Medical Association.*

868. Sharma, A., 1963, Mental retardation and education backwardness. *Guidance Review*, 1 : 133.

869. Sharma, B., Bajpai, P.C., and Sharma, N.L., 1972, Some observations of congenital malformations. *Indian Journal of Pediatrics*, 39 (296): 286-292.

870. Sharma, D.B., 1979, Community organisation for prevention of mental deficiency: A pediatricians view. *Indian Journal of Pediatrics*, 46 (377): 203-206.

871. Sharma, J.B., Gulati, N., and Malik, S., 1993, Acephalus acardia syndrome. *Indian Pediatrics*, 30 (2): 261-263.

872. Sharma, K.C., 1969, Population of the disabled: On the increase of disabilities and their new trends. *The Journal of Rehabilitation in Asia*, 10 : 13.

873. Sharma, N.L., Goel, K.M., Mehrotra, P.N., and Anand, J.S., 1964, The electrocardiogram and pseudohypertrophic muscular dystrophy. *Indian Journal of Pediatrics*, 31 (196): 145-150.

874. Sharma, N.L., Gowda, K.A., Goel, K.M., and Singh, R.N., 1965, A case of tuberous sclerosis. *Indian Journal of Pediatrics*, 32 (207): 135-138.

875. Sharma, N.L., Singh, R.N., and Anand, J.S., 1965, Hurler's syndrome. *Indian Journal of Pediatrics*, 32 (212): 301-306.

876. Sharma, N.L., and Dikshit, S.K., 1957, Some observations on the relationship of kwashiorkor and infantile liver cirrhosis. *Indian Journal of Pediatrics*, 24 (112): 169-178.

877. Sharma, P.D., 1970, The incidence of major congenital malformations in Mysore. *Indian Journal of Pediatrics*, 37 (275): 618-619.

878. Sharma, R., 1990, Rehabilitation management of mentally retarded amongst physically disabled. *Indian Journal of Physical Medicine and Rehabilitation*, 3 : 51-56.

879. Sharma, R.C., 1973, The effects of malnutrition on mental growth and mental health of the children. *Indian Journal of Psychiatry*, 15 : 272.

880. Sharma, R.C., and Suri, P.K., 1977, A report on phonology in language of a profoundly retarded. *Indian Journal of Mental Retardation*, 10 : 94.

881. Sharma, R.D., 1986, Puppet as creative arts for disabled. *IED Bulletin*, 4 (2): 48-53.

882. Sharma, S., 1973, Occupational TheRaoy: Its place in medical education for National Health Services. *The Journal of Rehabilitation in Asia*, 14 (2): 16-18.

883. Sharma, S.C., 1987, Physical education, physiotheRaoy, sports and yoga science influence the behavior of handicapped children. *Mind*, 13 (2): 14-19.

884. Sharma, T.R., 1987, A study of the symptoms and handling of mentally retarded child. *Indian Psychological Review*, 32 (4): 24-25.

885. Sharma, V., and Sharma, I.D., 1990, Universal presentation of trichobezoar. *Indian Pediatrics*, 27 (2): 187-189.

886. Sharma, V.P., 1976, Psychology and the developmentally handicapped. *Indian Journal of Mental Retardation*, 9 (1&2): 21-29.

887. Shastri, A.S.I., 1978, Counselling in mental illness and retrdation. *Social Welfare*, 24 : 11.

888. Shastri, A.S.I., and Misra, A.K., 1974, Assessment of social functioning of 56 mentally retarded children. *Indian Journal of Mental Retardation*, 7 (2): 31-35.

889. Sheshadri, S., Jain, S., and Maheshwari, M.C., 1990, Disability and rehabilitation in multiple sclerosis. *Indian Journal of Disability and Rehabilitation*, 4 (2): 31-43.

890. Sheth, G., and Jain, L., 1981, BM Institute of Mental Health: Philosophy and services. *Mental Health Review*.

891. Shetty, K.T., Sharma, N.L., and Wahal, K.M., 1966, Sex chromatin in mental retardation. *Indian Journal of Pediatrics*, 33 (216): 1-3.

892. Shetty, K.T., Sharma, N.L., and Wahal, K.M., 1966, Mongolism, lukemia and sex chromatin anomalies. *Indian Journal of Pediatrics*, 33 (219): 103-106.

893. Shrivastava, D.K., and Vesikar, S.S., 1965, Oxycephaly: A case report. *Indian Pediatrics*, 2 (3): 101-102.

894. Shukla, R.P., 1989, Special education: Identification of educationally handicapped children and non instructional responsibilities of teachers: Concept analysis and suggestions. *Indian Journal of Disability and Rehabilitation*, 3 (2): 73-80.

895. Shukla, R.S., Bhambull, S.S., and Bhandari, N.R., 1979, A study of superstitions and practices in under five. *Indian Pediatrics*, 16: 403-406.

896. Shukla, T.R., 1969, Mental subnormality and criminal behaviour. *Indian Journal of Mental Retardation*, 2 (2): 74-79.

897. Shukla, T.R., and Khoche, V., 1974, A study of adjustment problems in mentally retarded children. *Indian Journal of Mental Retardation*, 7 (1): 4-12.

898. Shukla, T.R., and Pershad, D., 1973, Rehabilitation of mentally retarded children. *Indian Journal of Mental Retardation,* 6 (1): 28-32.

899. Sidhar, S., 1970, How mentally retarded children can be helped?. *Social Welfare,* 16 : 13.

900. Sinclair, S., 1972, Etiological factors in mental retardation: A study of 470 cases. *Indian Pediatrics,* 9 : 391-396.

901. Sinclair, S., 1972, Familial mental retardation and parental consanguinity. *Indian Journal of Medical Research,* 60 (11): 1718-1723.

902. Sinclair, S., 1973, Counselling of parents of mentally retarded children. *Indian Pediatrics,* 10 : 115.

903. Sinclair, S., 1975, Information for parents of the retarded. *Indian Journal of Mental Retardation,* 8 : 43-47.

904. Sinclair, S., 1981, A future for the mentally handicapped. *Indian Journal of Public Administration,* 27 (3): 624.

905. Sinclair, S., 1981, New horizons in education for the mentally handicapped. *Indian Pediatrics,* 18 (12): 859-862.

906. Sinclair, S., 1981, A program for the mentally retarded. *The Journal of Rehabilitation in Asia,* 22 (4): 21-24.

907. Singh, A.K., 1988, Are the poor less intelligent? Or much ado about nothing?. *The Indian Journal of Social Work,* 49 (4): 377-380.

908. Singh, A.K., and Jaiswal, M., 1981, Correlates of scholastic achievement of socially disadvataged student. *Social Change,* 11 (1): 23-28.

909. Singh, A.N., 1973, Behavioural problems of the mentally retarded deaf. *Social Welfare,* 19 : 4.

910. Singh, D.N., 1988, Genes for Down's syndrome and Alzheimers disease share the same chromosomes 21. *Indian Journal of Pediatrics,* 55 (3): 352-353.

911. Singh, D.N., 1989, Parental detection of Down's syndrome in younger women. *Indian Journal of Pediatrics,* 56 (4): 458-462.

912. Singh, H., 1990, Determination of gestational age of newborns: A comparative study. *Indian Pediatrics,* 27 (11): 1229.

913. Singh, H., Ramakumar, L., and Gupta, H.L., 1967, Infantile spinal muscular atrophy. *Indian Journal of Pediatrics,* 34 (229): 34-38.

914. Singh, J.V., and Malik, G.K., 1979, Pyogenic meningitis: Some epidemiological observations. *Indian Journal of Pediatrics,* 46 (383): 437-440.

915. Singh, K.S.T., 1990, Trisomy 13 Pataus syndrome: A rare case of

survival into adulthood. *Journal of Mental Deficiency Research*, 34 : 91-93.

916. Singh, M., 1969, Some anatomical physiological and psychological peculiarities in infancy and childhood which cause parental anxiety but are of no significance. *Indian Journal of Pediatrics*, 36 (257): 226-227.

917. Singh, M., 1970, Feeding of low birth weight babies. *Indian Journal of Pediatrics*, 37 (275): 519-526.

918. Singh, M., 1977, Some practical aspects of neonatal jaundice. *Indian Journal of Pediatrics*, 44 (357): 215-219.

919. Singh, M., Giri, S.K., and Ramachandran, K., 1974, Intrauterine growth curves of live born babies. *Indian Journal of Pediatrics*, 41 : 475-479.

920. Singh, M., and Sharma, N.K., 1980, Spectrum of congenital malformations in the new born. *Indian Pediatrics*, 17 (386): 239-244.

921. Singh, M.V., 1972, Counselling needs of the parents of mentally retarded children. *Indian Journal of Pediatrics*, 39 (298): 361-363.

922. Singh, M.V., 1974, Some psychological correlates of mental subnormality. *Indian Journal of Mental Retardation*, 7 (1): 25-30.

923. Singh, M.V., 1979 Normalisation: Integration of the mentally subnormal individual into the community. *Indian Journal of Mental Retardation*, 12 (1&2): 12-17.

924. Singh, M.V., 1981, Parental participation in early detection of mental retardation. *Psyche-Care News*, 3 (5&6): 57-58.

925. Singh, M.V., 1983, Psychosocial assessment in mental retardation. *Child Psychiatry Quarterly*, 16 (3): 157-161.

926. Singh, M.V., Ananda, N.K., Gupta, S., and Dhingara, D.C., 1978, Intelligence in relation to degree of malnutrition. *Indian Journal of Clinical Psychology*, 5 (2): 117-120.

927. Singh, M.V., Ananda, N.K., Dhingara, D.C, and Gupta, S., 1976, Intelligence in relation to duration of protien caloric malnutrition. *Indian Journal of Psychiatry*, 18 : 52-54.

928. Singh, M.V., and Dagar, B., 1982, Sociological aspects of behaviour problems in a community child guidance centre. *Child Psychiatry Quarterly*, 15 (2): 43-49.

929. Singh, M.V., and Sahay, M., 1974, Mental health in children: Education and prevention. *Indian Journal of Pediatrics*, 41 (312): 19-21.

930. Singh, M.V., and Saini, L., 1974, Social class and mental

subnormality. *Indian Journal of Psychiatry,* 16 : 312.

931. Singh, N., 1990, Insecurity and anxiety levels of mothers of mentally retarded and normal children. *Journal of Personality and Clinical Studies,* 6 (1): 103-107.

932. Singh, R., and Kaushik, S.S., 1982, Parent training techniques in acquisition and generalisation of behaviour modification skill to train the retarded. *Indian Journal of Clinical Psychology,* 9 (2): 193-201.

933. Singh, R.P., and Sudharshan, P.S., 1981, Trichobezoar in acute intestinal obstruction. *Journal of Indian Medical Association,* p (3&4): 55-57.

934. Singh, R.R., 1975, Mentally retarded in Madhya Pradesh. *Social Welfare,* 21 : 23.

935. Singh, S., Dhall, J.L., Yadav, R., and Sekhon, G.S., 1978, Our experiences with spina bifida cystica. *Indian Journal of Pediatrics,* 45 (369): 323-327.

936. Singh, S.B., Nigam, A., and Srivastava, J.R., 1975, Some psychological characteristics of a Child Guidance Clinic intake. *Indian Journal of Pediatrics,* 42 (326): 79-86.

937. Singh, S.B., and Virmani, V., 1970, Perceptual disturbances in primary and secondary mental retardation with special reference to Bender-Gestalt and Draw a person test. *Indian Journal of Mental Retardation,* 3 (1): 40-49.

938. Singh, S.D., 1963, Craniofacial dystosis. *Indian Journal of Pediatrics,* 31 : 186.

939. Singh, S.D., Chhaparwal, B.C., Dhanda, R.P., and Pohowalla, J.N., 1970, A syndrome of dwarfism, mental retardation, lens opacities, nystagmus, strabismus, cryptorchidism and absent patellae. *Indian Journal of Pediatrics,* 37 (268): 197-199.

940. Singh, S.D., and Hussain, S., 1964, Heriditary cerebellar ataxia, mental deficiency, pyramidal involvement and macular pigmentation: A brief review with report of two cases. *Indian Journal of Pediatrics,* 31 (203): 355-358.

941. Singh, S.N., 1972, Educating and training of mental retardates. *Social Welfare,* 19 : 5.

942. Singh, U.B., 1972, The effect of institutionalisation on the performance of mentally retarded children. *The Journal of Rehabilitation in Asia,* 13 (4): 38-40.

943. Singh, V.K., 1973, Community health and mental retardation. *Indian Journal of Mental Retardation,* 6 (2): 97-101.

944. Singh, V.K., 1979, Problem children: Handicapped, maladjusted and mentally retarded. *Indian Psychological Review,* 18 (14): 122-128.

945. Singhal, P.K., Bhatia, M.S., Balkrishan, A., Dhar, N.K., Mullick, B.N., and Bohra, N., 1988, Psychiatric morbidity. *Indian Journal of Pediatrics,* 55 (4): 575-579.

946. Sinha, S., 1936, Learning curve of a mentally deficient child. *Indian Journal of Psychology,* 11 : 223-235.

947. Sinha, S.P., 1967, Effect of praise and reproof on paired associate learning in educationally retarded children. *Indian Journal of Experimental Psychology,* (1): 63-65.

948. Sinha, V., and Murari, P., 1982, Desired status in the family of mentally deficient children. *Research in Psychology,* 1 (1): 73-75.

949. Sircar, P.K., and Bharadwaj, B., 1973, Morbidity pattern among army personnel's children. *Indian Journal of Pediatrics,* 40 (311): 427-430.

950. Sitaram, M., 1984, Social integration of disabled children in ordinary schools. *The Journal of Rehabilitation in Asia,* 25 (3): 21-26.

951. Sitholey, P., Prasad, M., and Kumar, S.,1986, A study of government residential schools for the retarded children in Uttar Pradesh. *Indian Journal of Social Psychiatry,* 2 (4): 368-381.

952. Somasundaram, O., 1967, Syphilis and mental deficiency. *Indian Journal of Psychiatry,* 9, (2): 137-144.

953. Somasundaram, O., 1968, Some aetiological problems in mental retardation: Solved and unsolved. *Indian Pediatrics,* 5 p 145-148.

954. Somasundaram, O., 1968, Tuberous sclerosis: A review of Indian literature with a further report of four cases. *Indian Journal of Psychiatry,* 10 : 142.

955. Somasundaram, O., Papakumari, M., Jayanthum, V., and Kumar, M.S., 1983, Institutionalised mentally retarded in a state mental hospital. *Indian Journal of Psychiatry,* 25 (3): 180-184.

956. Somasundaram, O., Papakumari, M., Rajeswari, R., and Vijayalakshmi, S., 1976 Microcephaly. *Indian Journal of Pediatrics,* 43 : 21-27.

957. Somasundaram, O., and Kumar, M.S., 1984, Behaviour characteristics of the mentally retarded in a state mental hospital: A comparative study. *Indian Journal of Psychiatry,* 26 (2): 115-120.

958. Somasundaram, O., and Papakumari, M., 1973, Hartnup's disease: Report of two siblings. *Indian Pediatrics,* 10 : 455-458.

959. Somasundaram, O., and Papakumari, M., 1978, Down's syndrome cases in Madras city. *Indian Journal of Psychological Medicine,* 1 (1): 31-35.

960. Somasundaram, O., and Papakumari, M., 1979, Down's syndrome cases from Madras city: Their socio economic status. *Child Psychiatry Quarterly,* 12 (2): 43-47.

961. Somasundaram, O., and Papakumari, M., 1981, A study of Down's anomaly. *Child Psychiatry Quarterly,* 14 (3): 85-94.

962. Somasundaram, O., and Vaidyalingam, M., 1966, Tuberous sclerosis: A report of 12 cases. *Indian Journal of Psychiatry,* 8 (4): 311-325.

963. Sood, M., Kumar, S., Kashyap, N., Berry, M., Bhargava, S., and Hingorani, V., 1987, Etiology factors and parental risk in symmetrical and asymmetrical intrauterine growth retardation. *Indian Journal of Pediatrics,* 54 (6): 926-929.

964. Sood, S.C., and Goyal, B.G., 1969, An unusual form of progressive muscular dystrophy: Case report. *Indian Journal of Pediatrics,* 36 (257): 219-222.

965. Srikantia, S.G., Venkatachalam, P.S., Reddy, V., and Gopalan, C., 1964, Protien calorie needs in kwashiorkor. *Indian Journal of Medical Research,* 52 (6): 1104.

966. Srikantia, S.G., and Gopalan, C., 1959, Renal function in nutritional oedema. *Indian Journal of Medical Research,* 47 (4): 467-471.

967. Srinivas, K.N., 1977, School behaviour of retarded children. *Special Education in India,* 1 (1): 44-45.

968. Sriramachary, S., and Ramalingaswami, V., 1953, Liver changes in kwashiorkor. *Indian Journal of Pediatrics,* 20 : 1-6.

969. Srivastava, A.K., Agarwal, V.K., Gupta, S.K., and Mehrotra, S.N., 1978, A longitudinal study of physical growth and morbidity pattern of small for date babies from birth to six months of age. *Indian Journal of Pediatrics,* 45 (360): 1-10.

970. Srivastava, G., 1969, Pyogenic meningitis. *Indian Journal of Pediatrics,* 36 (260): 307-313.

971. Srivastava, J.R., Srivastava, V.K., Mehrotra, S.N., and Samuel, K.C., 1968, Clinical and bacteriological study of pyogenic menigitis in children. *Indian Journal of Pediatrics,* 35 : 1.

972. Srivastava, J.R., and Gupta, S., 1958, Oxycephaly. *Indian Journal of Pediatrics,* 25 : 122 : 112-115.

973. Srivastava, N., 1970, The setting and adjustment problems of children in a school for the retarded: A preliminary report. *Indian Journal of Mental Retardation,* 3 (1): 80-86.

974. Srivastava, R., and Alam, R.G., 1986, Recall of pictures and words in PAT of normal and educable retardates employing stimulus generated and E supplied strategies. *Indian Psychological Review,* 30 (5): 17-20.

975. Srivastava, R.K., 1978, Attitudes of mothers of mentally retarded children towards certain aspects of child rearing patterns. *Indian Journal of Mental Retardation,* 11 (2): 64-74.

976. Srivastava, R.K., 1990, Frustration aggression patterns of mothers of retarded children. *Disabilities and Impairments,* 4 (1): 51-56.

977. Srivastava, R.K., Seth, M., and Shobha, S., 1981, Maternal personality pattern of educable mentally retarded children on Cattell's 16 PF test. *Child Psychiatry Quarterly,* 14 (3): 100-107.

978. Srivastava, S.P., 1968, Job placement of the mentally retarded. *Indian Journal of Mental Retardation,* 1 (2): 81-86.

979. Srivastava, S.P., 1971, Social work tasks in a team for the rehabilitation of the mentally retarded children. *Indian Journal of Mental Retardation,* 4 (1&2): 34-44.

980. Srivastava, S.P., 1971, The challenge of mental retardation: On teaching trades to them. *Social Welfare,* 17 : 6.

981. Subbegowda, S.K., Narayanan, H.S., Padmashree, S., and Rao, B.S.S.R., 1987 Studies on Down's syndrome and maternal age. *Indian Journal of Psychiatry,* 29 (1): 77-79.

982. Subrahmanyan, V., Doraiswamy, T.R., Joseph, T., Rao, N.N., and Swaminathan, M., 1957, Treatment of nutritional oedema syndrome, kwashiorkor, with a low cost protein food. *Indian Journal of Pediatrics,* 24 (110): 112-115.

983. Subramanyam, G., 1972, Religion for the mentally retarded. *Special Education in India,* 1 (1): 50-52.

984. Subramanyan, G., Agarwal, K.N., Agarwal, S.P., and Jaiswal, A., 1974, Clinical and aetiological study of childhood mental retardation. *Indian Pediatrics,* 11 : 723.

985. Sudha, B.C., 1981, The value of sports and recreation for mentally retarded. *The Nursing Journal of India,* 60 (3): 63.

986. Sudha, T., Jayam, S., and Ramachandran, R., 1990, The association of 13q 14q with Down's syndrome and its inheritance. *Indian Journal of Pediatrics,* 57 (2): 249-252.

987. Sultana, Z., Talib, V.H., Patil, S.D., Magar, D.N., and Sharma, K.D., 1975, Congenital malformations: An autopsy study. *Journal of Obstetrics and Gyneacology,* 25 : 329.

988. Sur, A.M., Chakravarthy, A., and Sharma, K.D., 1959, Tuberculous meningitis. *Indian Journal of Child Health,* 8 (5): 281.

989. Surya, N.C., 1964, Psychiatric morbidity in Pondicherry. *Transactions of All India Institute for Mental Health,* 4.

990. Swaminathan, M.L., Jothi, K.K., Singh, R., Madhavan, S., and Gopalan, C., 1964, Semi longitudinal study of growth and related factors. *Indian Pediatrics,* 1 : 255.

991. Swaminathan, S., 1988, Congenital leukemia in an infant with Down syndrome. *Indian Journal of Pediatrics,* 55 (1): 142-144.

992. Swarna, M., Rao D.N., Kumari, C.K., and Reddy, P.P., 1981, Hydroxyprolinemia: A Case report. *Indian Journal of Pediatrics,* 48, (4): 527-528.

993. Takrani, L.B., 1969, Psuedo-mental retardation. *Indian Journal of Mental Retardation,* 2 (2): 87-97.

994. Tandon, L., Gupta, S.P., and Dikshit, S.K., 1971, A study of some physical criteria for the assessment of prematurity. *Indian Journal of Pediatrics,* 38 (279): 187-201.

995. Tandon, P., Jha, S., Tandon, R., Sonidhi, D., Chandra, M., and Trivedi, J.K., 1990, Orodental patterns in mentally retarded. *Indian Journal of Psychiatry,* 32 (2): 185-187.

996. Taneja, B.L., Wanchop S.N., and Dutta, R.N., 1955, Histological study of encephalitis in northern India. *Indian Journal of Medical Research,* 43 (4): 775-782.

997. Taneja, P.N., and Ghai, O.P., 1955, Pyogenic meningitis in children. *Indian Journal of Pediatrics,* 22 (91): 99-106.

998. Tangavelu, M., 1981, Administration for the disabled: Policy and organisational issues. *Indian Journal of Public Administration,* 27 (3): 537-545.

999. Tangri, P., and Verma, P., 1992, A study of social burden felt by mother's of handicapped children. *Journal of Personality and Clinical Studies,* 8 (1&2): 117-120.

1000. Taskar. K.T., 1974, Welfare of the blind and the mentally handicapped. *Social Welfare,* 21 : 66.

1001. Taylor, A.M., 1972, A programme of recreation and physical education. *Special Education in India,* 1 (1): 34-35.

1002. Teja, J.S., 1969, Problems in classifying the retarded, Editorial, *Indian Journal of Mental Retardation,* 2 (2): 66-67.

1003. Teja, J.S., Shah, D.K., and Verma, S.K., 1970, A comparative study of motor and social milestones and their relationship with intelligence test results in the mental retardates. *Indian Journal of Mental Retardation,* 3 (1): 75-79.

1004. Teja, J.S., Verma, S.K., and Shah, D.K., 1971, A comparative study of the background factors in mentally retarded and emotionally disturbed children. *Indian Journal of Mental Retardation,* 4 (1&2): 4-9.

1005. Teotia, M., Teotia, S.P.S., Sharma, N.L., and Kunwar, K.B., 1972, Fat absorption studies in kwashiorkor. *Indian Journal of Medical Research,* 60 (4): 620-627.

1006. Teotia, M., Teotia, S.P.S., and Sharma, N.L., 1967, Fat balance studies in marasmus. *Indian Journal of Medical Research,* 55 (1): 12.

1007. Teotia, M., Teotia, S.P.S. and Singh, R.K., 1977, Rickets in tuberous sclerosis from ant convulsant drugs. *Indian Journal of Pediatrics,* 44 (357): 227-231.

1008. Thaper, R.K., 1967, Incidence of positive bacteriology in cases of tuberculous meningitis in children. *Indian Pediatrics,* 4 (4): 169-194.

1009. Thaper, U., 1986, Creative art: As an aid in education for mentally retarded. *IED Bulletin,* 4 (2): 40-47.

1010. Thaper, U., 1987, Creative art for the mentally retarded: As as educational aid. *IED Bulletin,* 5 (2): 24-31.

1011. Thomas, S., Menon, P.S.N., and Khan, M.A., 1983, Mucopolysaccharidoses VI: Maroteaux Lamy syndrome. *Indian Pediatrics,* 20 : 378.

1012. Thressiakutty, A.T., 1991, Open employment opportunities in the Indian railways for persons with mental retardation. *Indian Journal of Disability and Rehabilitation,* 5 (1): 1-11.

1013. Thressiakutty, A.T., Narayan, J., and Menon, D.K., 1988, Systematic training and job placement of persons with mental retardation: A Model. *Indian Journal of Disability and Rehabilitation,* 2 : 25-34.

1014. Thressiakutty, A.T., and Narayan, J., 1990, Parental perceptions of problems and expectations regarding their mentally retarded children. *Indian Journal of Disability and Rehabilitation,* 4 (2): 54-63.

1015. Tilou. A., 1976, Intermediate section of the educable mentally handicapped. *Special Education in India,* 1 (1) 24-26.

1016. Tiwari, J.N., 1981, National Sample Survey, NSS, of the disabled in India. *Indian Journal of Public Administration,* 27 (3): 779.

1017. Trivedi, C.R., and Mavalankar, D.V., 1986, Epidemiology of low birth weight in Ahmedabad. *Indian Journal of Pediatrics,* 53 (6): 795-800.

1018. Udani, P.M., 1954, Muscle changes in malnutrition and syndrome of nutritional myelopathy in children. *Indian Journal of Child*

Health, 3 (4): 167-177.

1019. Udani, P.M., 1962, Kwashiorkor myelopathy. *Indian Journal of Child Health,* 11 (10): 498-501.

1020. Upadhyay, R.K., 1971, Counselling the parents of mentally handicapped children. *Social Welfare,* 18 : 7.

1021. Upadhyay, R.K., 1972, A study of public opinion towards rehabilitation of mental patients. *The Journal of Rehabilitation in Asia,* 13 (4): 33-36.

1022. Upadhyaya, S., and Sinha, A.K., 1974, Some findings on psychodiognostic tests with young retarded adults. *Indian Journal of Clinical Psychology,* 1 (2): 73-79.

1023. Valiualla, S., 1991, Some experiences and observations of yoga programme with mentally handicapped. *Mental Health Review,* 5 (2): 32-40.

1024. Varadkar, A.M., Mahali, S.D., and Patel, Z.M., 1983, GM3 Gangliosidoses Type 2, Sandhoff's disease. *Indian Pediatrics,* 20: 302.

1025. Vare, A.M., and Bansal, P.C., 1971, Anencephaly: An anatomical study of 41 anencephalics. *Indian Journal of Pediatrics,* 33 (281): 197-205.

1026. Varkki, C., Venkatachalam, P.S., Srikantia, S.G., and Gopalan, S., 1955, Study of birth weights of infants in relation to incidence of nutritional oedema syndrome,Kwashiorkor, *Indian Journal of Medical Research,* 43 (2): 291-296.

1027. Varma, B.M., and Agarwal, V.K., 1966, Ocular manifestations of tuberculous meningitis in children: A clinical study. *Indian Pediatrics,* 3 (5): 187-89.

1028. Varma, J., 1986, Special education in India: A critical analysis of the present status with special reference to mental retardation. *Perspectives in Psychological Researches,* 9, (1): 42-46.

1029. Varma, R.K., 1981, Preventive measures in handicapped children. *Journal of Indian Dental Association,* 53 (6): 173-174.

1030. Varma, S.C., and Varma, C.K., 1974, Integrating mentally retarded with normal children: An experiment. *Indian Journal of Mental Retardation,* 7 : 81-85.

1031. Varma, V.K., Mangalwedhe, K.P., and Misra, A.K., 1976, A comparison of sociodemographic treatment and follow up of variables of mentally retarded and emotionally disturbed children. *Child Psychiatry Quarterly,* 9 : 1-5.

1032. Vashi, N., and Joshi, A., 1968, The changing pattern of purulent meningitis. *Indian Pediatrics,* 5 : 444.

1033. Veeraraghavan, V., 1982, Education of the mentally retarded: Certain issues. *Indian Journal of Mental Retardation*, 15 (1): 19-29.

1034. Veeraraghavan, V., 1987, Integrated education for mental retardates. *Disabilities and Impairments*, 1 (1&2): 80-83.

1035. Venkatachalam, P.S., Srikantia, S.G., Mehta, F., and Gopalan, C., 1956, Treatment of nutritional oedema syndrome, Kwashiorkor, with vegetable protein diets. *Indian Journal of Medical Research*, 44 (3): 539.

1036. Venkatachalam, P.S., Srikantia, S.G., and Gopalan, C., 1952, Nutritional oedema in children. *Indian Journal of Pediatrics*, 19: 165.

1037. Venkatachalam, P.S., Srikantia, S.G., and Gopalan, C., 1954, Clinical features of nutritional oedema syndrome. *Indian Journal of Medical Research*, 42 (3): 555.

1038. Venkatachalam, P.S., and Gopalan, P.C., 1960, Kwashiorkor in Hyderabad and Coonoor: A comparison of salient features. *Indian Journal of Medical Research*, 48 (5): 645.

1039. Venkatesan, S., 1991, Bender Gestalt Visuo Motor Test as a measure of intelligence in mentally handicapped individuals. *Indian Journal of Clinical Psychology*, 18 (1): 7-9.

1040. Venkatesan, S., 1991, Psychological assessment of individuals with mental retardation: Some perspectives and problems. *Creative Psychologist*, 3 (2): 65-75.

1041. Venkatesan, S.,1993, Recent trends in behavioural assessment of individuals with mental handicap in India. *The Creative Psychologist.*

1042. Venkatesan, S., and Rao, P.M., 1990, Validity of parental estimates against actual test estimates in mentally handicapped individuals. *The Creative Psychologist* 2 (2): 71-75.

1043. Venkatesan, S., and Reddy, K.R., 1990, Idiometric approaches to functional assessment in mentally handicapped adults: Report of a pilot study. *Indian Journal of Clinical Psychology*, 17 (1): 21-27.

1044. Venkatesan, S., and Reddy, K.R., 1991, Validation of an idiometrically based functional assessment battery for mentally handicapped adults. *Indian Journal of Clinical Psychology*, 18 (1): 31-34.

1045. Venkatesan, S., and Reddy, K.R., 1992, Sensitivity of an idiometrically based functional assessment battery to changes in neuropsychological functions in adults with mental handicap. *The*

Creative Psychologist, 4 (1): 7-11.

1046. Venkatesan, S., and Vepuri, V.G.D., 1992, Perceived patterns of Adjustment in adults with mental retardation. *The Creative Psychologist,* 4 (2): 63-68.

1047. Venkatesan, S., and Vepuri, V.G.D., 1992, Parental perception of causes and management of problem behaviours in individuals with mental handicap. *Disabilities and Impairments,* 7 (2): 29-37.

1048. Vepuri, V.G.D., Venkatesan, S., and Sivakumar, T.C., 1992, Perception of work behaviours by vocational instructors in adults with mental retardation. *Journal of Personality and Clinical Studies,* 8 (2): 111-115.

1049. Verghese, A., 1984, Problems encountered in rehabilitating the mentally disabled. *The Journal of Rehabilitation in Asia,* 25 (2): 25-30.

1050. Verghese, A., Baig, A., Senseman, L.A., Rao, P.S.S.S., and Benjamin, V., 1973, A social and psychiatric study of a representative group of families in Vellore town. *Indian Journal of Medical Research,* 61 (3): 608.

1051. Verghese, A., Baig, A., and Abraham, A., 1976, Social class and psychiatric disturbance: A community study. *Indian Journal of Medical Research,* 64 (11): 1672-1676.

1052. Verghese, A., and Baig, A., 1974 Psychiatric disturbance in children: An epidemiological study. *Indian Journal of Medical Research,* 62 (10): 1538-1542.

1053. Verghese, A., and Rao, D.L.N.M., 1961, Mongolism: A review of some aspects. *Transactions of All India Institute for Mental Health,* 2 (1): 1-17.

1054. Verma, B.,S and Tailor, M.H., 1965, Familial tuberous sclerosis: A review of three cases. *Indian Pediatrics,* 2 (11): 401-410.

1055. Verma, I.C., 1970, Dermatoglyphics in clinical pediatrics. *Indian Journal of Pediatrics,* 37 (275): 583-589.

1056. Verma, I.C., 1970, Cornelia De Lange Syndrome: Report of a case. *Indian Journal of Pediatrics,* 37 (267): 152-154.

1057. Verma, I.C., 1974, Homocystenuria: Report of two cases in siblings. *Indian Pediatrics,* 11 : 753-755.

1058. Verma, I.C., 1981, A place in the sun for the disabled so that they may also live: A perspective on International Year for Disabled Persons, IYDP, *Indian Journal of Pediatrics,* 48 : 689-696.

1059. Verma, I.C., 1988, Mucopolysaccharide disorders in India: A commentary. *Indian Journal of Pediatrics,* 55 (6): 999-1002.

1060. Verma, I.C., 1990, Cytogenetic analysis of Down's syndrome.

Indian Journal of Pediatrics, 57 (2): 245-248.

1061. Verma, I.C and Ghai, O.P., 1970, Pediatrics and the human chromosomes: A review. *Indian Journal of Pediatrics*, 37 (265): 28-43.

1062. Verma, I.C., Gupta, A.K., and Devanagondi, B.S., 1975, Downs syndrome: Maternal age in 615 cases in India and its implication in genetic counselling. *Indian Pediatrics*, 12 : 1239.

1063. Verma, I.C., Malhotra, A.K., Malik, G.R., and Ghai, O.P., 1979, Cytogenetic profile of Down s syndrome in India. *Indian Journal of Medical Research*, 68 : 147-151.

1064. Verma, I.C., and Ghai, O.P., 1971, Hypothyroidism in children with mongolism. *Indian Journal of Pediatrics*, 38 (280): 229-232.

1065. Verma, I.C., and Gupta, A.K., 1975, Down's syndrome: Maternal age in 615 cases in India and its implications in genetic counselling. *Indian Pediatrics*, 12 : 1239-1248.

1066. Verma, I.C., and Sinclair, S., 1970, Homocystinuria. *Indian Journal of Pediatrics*, 37 (259): 263-267.

1067. Verma, S.K., 1968, Research and rehabilitation projects of mental retardation at Nandavan, Nagpur. *Indian Journal of Mental Retardation*, 1 (1): 49-52.

1068. Verma, S.K., 1971, Intelligence assessment in the mentally retardates: Some experiences. *Indian Journal of Mental Retardation*, 4 (1&2): 10-14.

1069. Verma, S.K., 1971, Poverty and mental retardation. *The Journal of Rehabilitation in Asia*, 12 (1): 42-44.

1070. Verma, S.K., 1973, The retardates and their families, Editorial, *Indian Journal of Mental Retardation*, 6 (2): 49-50.

1071. Verma, S.K., 1979, An analysis of 76 Down's syndrome referrals. *Journal of Rajasthan Psychiatric Society*.

1072. Verma, S.K., 1983, Leisure acitvities and handicapped persons. *Bombay Psychologist*, 5 (1) 24-28.

1073. Verma, S.K., 1991, On going research studies at the Rehabilitation Centre of the BM Institute of Mental Health: 1991-1992. *Mental Health Review*, 5 (2): 41-44.

1074. Verma, S.K., Pershad, D., and Menon, R.P., 1979, Cross validation of Developmental Screening Test. *Indian Journal of Clinical Psychology*, 6 (1): 17-20.

1075. Verma, S.K., Pershad, D., and Randhawa, A., 1979, The preliminary report on a performance test of intelligence on 4-8 year old children. *Indian Journal of Clinical Psychology*, 6 (2): 125-130.

1076. Verma, S.K., Pershad, D., and Randhawa, A., 1980, Are Indian children slow? Report of an enquiry with a special measure of intelligence. *Child Psychiatry Quarterly,* 13 (3): 67-71.

1077. Verma, S.K., Shah, O.K., and Teja, J.S., 1970, Brain damaged child: Psychometric aspects. *Indian Journal of Mental Retardation,* 3 (1): 87-121.

1078. Verma, S.K., and Pershad, D., and Kaushal, P., 1972, Gessell drawing test as a measure of intelligence in the mentally retarded children. *Indian Journal of Mental Retardation,* 5 (1&2): 64-68.

1079. Verma, S.K., and Teja, J.S., 1971, Backward child. *The Bombay Hospital Journal,* 13 (1): 6-8.

1080. Verma, S.K., and Valiualla, S., 1981, Down's syndrome and other mentally retarded referrals: A study of certain variables. *Child Psychiatry Quarterly,* 14 (3): 64-71.

1081. Verma, V.K., and Seshadri, M., 1989, Intervention programmes for parents of mentally retarded children. *Annals of National Academy for Medical Sciences,India,* 25 (1): 309-318.

1082. Verma, V.P., 1978, Social integration of the handicapped. *Social Welfare,* 27 (7): 10.

1083. Vohra, R., 1988, Institutional services for the disabled: Series II. *Disabilities and Impairments,* 2 (1): 59-81.

1084. Vohra, R., and Bahadur, I., 1981, Transfer of training in mentally retarded and normal children. *Indian Journal of Mental Retardation,* 14 (1): 26-39.

1085. Vyas, B.M., Chaturvedi, M.K., Joshi, R.C., Joshi, N., and Stija, D.C., 1978, Tuberous sclerosis: A report of two cases. *Indian Journal of Psychiatry,* 20, (3): 281-282.

1086. Vyas, K.J., 1957, Tuberculous meningitis. *Indian Journal of Child Health,* 6 (12): 853.

1087. Vyas, K.J., 1964, Macrodactyly: A case report. *Indian Journal of Pediatrics,* 31 (195): 117.

1088. Wadkar, A.J., and Palsane, M.N., 1978, Diagnosing mental retardation in the slow pupil. *Indian Journal of Mental Retardation,* 11 (2): 49-63.

1089. Warde, S., 1991, Impact of mental disability on family. *Pediatric Clinics of India,* 20 : 47-58.

1090. Warey, P., Tarmer, S.K., Agarwal, S.K., and Chaturvedi, V., 1983, Niemann Pick disease. *Indian Pediatrics,* 20 : 613.

1091. Warrier, C.B.C., 1965, Infantile spasms,salaam seizures,: A case report. *Indian Pediatrics,* 2 (12): 460-463.

1092. Wig, N.N., Mehta, M., and Sahasi, G., 1985, A study of time utilisation and perceived burden of mentally handicapped child in joint and nuclear families. *Indian Journal of Social Psychiatry,* 1 : 251-261.

1093. Wig, N.N., Mehta, S., and Verma, S.K., 1981, Methodological shortcomings of previous studies on malnutrition and mental development. *Asian Journal of Psychology and Education,* 8 : 25.
1094. Wig, N.N., Shah, D.K., and Verma, H.C., 1969, Brain damaged child: A clinical study of fifty cases. *Indian Journal of Mental Retardation,* 2 (1): 15-20.
1095. Xavier, S., 1974, Special classes for the retarded. *The Journal of Rehabilitation in Asia,* 15 (3): 10-13.

PHYSICAL HANDICAP

1096. Agarwal, A.K., Sharma, V.P., Kacker, J.N., Sharma, R.K., Jain, U.K., and Goyal, M.K., 1984, A clinical study of congenital limb deficiencies. *The Journal of Rehabilitation in Asia,* 25, (1): 33-43.
1097. Agarwal, A.K., Sharma, V.P., Singh, O.P., Kumar, R., Singhal, A.K., and Mishra, U.S., 1990, A follow up study of usefulness of wheel chair: Preliminary report, *Indian Journal of Physical Medicine and Rehabilitation,* 3 (1): 41-44.
1098. Agarwal, A.K., Sharma, V.P., and Mishra, V.S., 1988, Prevalence of physical disability in India with special reference to amputation. *Indian Journal of Disability and Rehabilitation,* 2 : 1-10.
1099. Agarwal, A.K., Varma, S., Sharma, V.P., Srivastava, R.P., Rastogi, S., and Goyal, M.K., 1984, A clinico respiratory study of spinal cord injury patients. *The Journal of Rehabilitation in Asia,* 25 (1): 15-19.
1100. Agarwal, S., and Verma, ., 1992, Grass root approach linkages and management of physically disabled children. *Disabilities and Impairments,* 4 5 (1&2): 22-27.
1101. Amesur, C.A., 1961, Education and welfare of the physically handicapped. *Nirmal Seva,* 1 : 1.
1102. Arya, A., Pershad, D., and Das, K., 1984, Psychosocial functioning in amputees. *The Journal of Rehabilitation in Asia,* 25 (2): 31-36.
1103. Ashoke, S., and Narayan, D.B., 1980, Rehabilitation of the congenitally deficit hand. *The Journal of Rehabilitation in Asia,* 21 (1): 31-35.
1104. Azhar, A.S., Kumar, R., Srivastava, A.K., Rehman, H., and Agarwal, K., 1980, Outcome of poliomyelitis in Allahabad. *Journal of Indian Academy of Pediatrics,* 17 : 751-760.

1105. Bajpai, J., Verma, A.N., and Sharma, J.M., 1984, A evaluation of functional efficiency of hand following fracture of fore arm bones using grip strength method. *The Journal of Rehabilitation in Asia,* 25 (2): 10-17.

1106. Balakrishnan, A., 1980, Tilting stubbies: An interchangeable plan for bilateral above knee amputees. *The Journal of Rehabilitation in Asia,* 21 (1): 41-47.

1107. Balakrishnan, A., 1986, An orthosis for barefoot walking. *The Journal of Rehabilitation in Asia,* 27 (2): 20-21.

1108. Balme, H., 1951, Treatment and after care of physically handicapped children. *The Indian Journal of Social Work,* 11 4, 365-371.

1109. Bandyopadhya, A.K., and Mirajkar, T.P., 1984, Solving the problem of a congenital lower limb deformed child with prothesis. *The Journal of Rehabilitation in Asia,* 25 (1): 44-51.

1110. Banerjee, G.R., 1951, Social case worker and physically handicapped child. *The Indian Journal of Social Work,* 11 (4): 362-380.

1111. Basu, R.W., 1981, Magnitude of problem of poliomyelitis in India. *Indian Pediatrics,* 18 (8): 507-511.

1112. Basu, S.N., 1970, Poliomyelitis, review article, *Indian Journal of Pediatrics,* 37 (266): 118-123.

1113. Bole, V.S., Gujral, V.V., and Singh, J.M., 1973, Rehabilitation of Volkman's Ischaemic contracture in children: A report of 12 cases. *The Journal of Rehabilitation in Asia,* 14 (3): 15-19.

1114. Bose, S., and Banerjee, S.N., 1969, A resolution on the personality make up of some institutionalised physically handicapped children by the Children's Apperception Test, CAT, *Journal of Psychological Researches,* 13 (1): 32-36.

1115. Chand, S., Sengwan, S.S., and Khatri, C.R., 1992, Post polio residual paralysis. *Indian Journal of Disability and Rehabilitation,* 6 (1): 33-38.

1116. Chandola, R.D., 1969, A beacon of hope for India's handicapped: Prosthetic workshop, a meeting place of art and industry. *Social Welfare,* 15 (5): 31.

1117. Chandra, K., 1978, Accident proneness in the orthopedically handicapped in comparison to normals. *The Journal of Rehabilitation in Asia,* 19 (2): 16-17.

1118. Chandra, K., 1980, Vocational rehabilitation of physically handicapped: A comprehensive study. *The Journal of Rehabilitation in Asia,* 21 (3): 42-49.

1119. Chitre, R.G., and Agashi, S., 1956, Metabolic studies in poliomyelitis. *Indian Journal of Medical Research,* 44 (4): 609-618.

1120 Chittibabu, A., 1978, Sudeks' atrophy and physical theRaoy: A clinical study. *The Journal of Rehabilitation in Asia,* 19 (3): 12-14.

1121. Chopra, R.M., 1977, Employment situation and educational levels of the orthopedically handicapped. *The Indian Journal of Social Work,* 38 (3): 269-273.

1122. Das, A.K., 1958, A review of post polio paralysis in children. *Indian Journal of Pediatrics,* 25 (126): 395-405.

1123. Das, S.K., Barik, R.K., and Nanda, A.N., 1990, Management of gross shortening of lower extremity by extension prosthesis. *Indian Journal of Disability and Rehabilitation,* 4 (1): 39-44.

1124. Deb, M., 1967, Personality pattern of post-polio paralysis: A psychoanalytical approach. *Samiksha,* 21 (3): 131-138.

1125. Deshmukh, A., and Rawat, B., 1977, Domestic management of acute poliomyelitis in a rural set up. *The Journal of Rehabilitation in Asia,* 18 (2): 18-20.

1126. Gandhi, P.K., 1976, Rehabilitation of the physically handicapped: Some social psychological considerations. *Social Work Forum,* 13 (4): 14-17.

1127. Ganesan, V., 1982, Vocational rehabilitation of the amputees: Satisfactoriness. *The Journal of Rehabilitation in Asia,* 23 (3): 16-20.

1128. Ghosh, B.N., Haldar, A., and Das, K.K., 1982, Prevalence of physically handicapped in an urban slum community detected through different categories of health personnel, Survey Methods, *Indian Journal of Public Health,* 26 (3): 187-193.

1129. Goel, S.C., Sharma, S.V., Singh, H.P., and Prasad, A., 1990, Poliomyelitis: A study of 500 cases. *Indian Journal of Physical Medicine and Rehabilitation,* 3 (1): 37-40.

1130. Gon, M., and Advani, B.B.K., 1983, Locus of control in orthopedically handicapped and non-handicapped persons. *Journal of Psychological Researches,* 27 (2): 75-80.

1131. Gujral, V.V., 1965, Nivalin in the treatment of residual post polio paralysis and pseudo-hypertrophic muscular dystrophy. *Indian Pediatrics,* 2 (3): 89-93.

1132. Gupta, A., Pedi, K., Rege P.V., Ramadas, G., and Athani, B.D., 1992, Functional assessment of driving skills in locomotor handicapped. *Indian Journal of Disability and Rehabilitation,* 6 (1): 15-24.

1133. Gupta, A.L., and Sachdeva, K.C., 1973, Rehabilitation of congenital amputees of the lower limb. *The Journal of Rehabilitation in Asia,* 14 (1): 11-14.

1134. Gupta, P.C., Gathwala, G., Aneja, S., and Arora, S.K., 1990, Acute cereballar ataxia: An unusual presentation of poliomyelitis. *Indian Pediatrics,* 27 (6): 622-623.

1135. Ismail, F., 1960, Services for the physically handicapped. *The Indian Journal of Social Work,* 21 (4): 86-94.

1136. Jain, S., and Delisa, J.A., 1988, CAD-CAM in the design of lower limb prosthetics. *Indian Journal of Disability and Rehabilitation,* 2 : 17-22.

1137. Joshi, J.B., Chandrakanta, C., and Verma, S.K., 1979, Comparison of muscle recovery in poliomyelitis in patients receiving regular physiotheRaoy at home or in the hospital. *Indian Journal of Pediatrics,* 46 (379): 266-273.

1138. Joshi, R.M., 1985, Congenital limb defects. *Journal of the Indian Academy of Pediatrics,* 22 : 107.

1139. Kalla, A.K., and Yadav, B.B., 1979, Periarthritis shoulder: A clinical study. *The Journal of Rehabilitation in Asia,* 20, (2): 24-28.

1140. Kesar, S., 1974, Problems in using public transport by the physically handicapped. *The Journal of Rehabilitation in Asia,* 15 (1): 13-16.

1141. Kumar, A.K.R., Bajpayee, A.K., and Agarwal, A.K., 1989, A clinical study of 588 rural based locomotor disabled: Camp study. *Indian Journal of Physical Medicine and Rehabilitation,* 2;29-32.

1142. Kumar, K., and Kapathia, N.K., 1988, Pattern of involvement in lower limbs in poliomyelitis. *Indian Journal of Orthopedics,* 22 : 138-143.

1143. Kumar, R., and Arun, S.M.,1981, Study of poliomyelitis in 123 cases. *The Journal of Rehabilitation in Asia,* 22 (2): 33-36.

1144. Kumar, R., Jawaid, S.M., and Arun, S.M., 1984, Role of physiotheRaoy in Bell's palsy. *The Journal of Rehabilitation in Asia,* 25 (1): 20-25.

1145. Kumar, R., and Arun, S.M., 1979, Ice theRaoy in the management of extra articular ankylosis of the knee. *The Journal of Rehabilitation in Asia,* 20 (3): 17-20.

1146. Lal, S.K., Verma, S.K., Yadav, B.P., and Joshi, J.B., 1970, A clinical study of 100 patients with poliomyelitis. *Indian Journal of Pediatrics,* 37 (275): 504-508.

1147. Mani, M.P., 1980, Social case work and the physically handicapped children. *The Journal of Rehabilitation in Asia,* 21 (3): 36-38.

1148. Marwah, V., and Shamimuddin, M.K., 1972, An experimental upper limb prosthesis for short shoulder stump. *The Journal of Rehabilitation in Asia,* 13 (3): 14-15.

1149. Meenakshi, P., 1981, Physical handicap: The problem of definition. *Indian Journal of Public Administration,* 27 (3): 666.

1150. Mehrotra, K.K., 1981, Scope of research in psychology of adjustment to physical disability. *The Journal of Rehabilitation in Asia,* 22 (1) 8-10.

1151. Mehta, M., 1981, Clinical psychology in the care of the physically handicapped. *Psyche-Care News,* 3 : 43-44.

1152. Mehta, S.P., Rai, S.L., and Patel, S.A., 1985, Early mobilisation in dorsal and lumbar spine injuries with cord involvement: A clinical study. *The Journal of Rehabilitation in Asia,* 26 (2): 37-43.

1153. Menon, P.B.M., 1980, Subcuteneous sympathetic block at the wrist level for functional restoration of the hand reflects dystrophy. *The Journal of Rehabilitation in Asia,* 21 (1): 36-41.

1154. Mittal, R.L., Bedi, G.P.S., and Gulati, A., 1987, A follow up study of above knee prosthesis manufactured in Artificial Limb Centre, Rajendra Hospital, Patiala. *The Journal of Rehabilitation in Asia,* 28 (1): 5-9.

1155. Mittal, R.L., and Singla, V.K., 1987, Forearm amputees of rural Punjab and their rehabilitation. *The Journal of Rehabilitation in Asia,* 28 (2): 1-5.

1156. Mohanty, P.R., Satoathy, S.K., and Rothi, S.B., 1984, An epidemiological study of post paralytic poliomyeletic cases in Pondicherry. *The Journal of Rehabilitation in Asia,* 25 (3) 39-45.

1157. Moses, M.S., 1974, Role of medical social workers in the rehabilitation of the physically handicapped person. *The Indian Journal of Social Work,* 34 (4): 295-306.

1158. Mukherji, A.K., and Rao, V.G.R., 1980, Management of lower limb amputees. *The Journal of Rehabilitation in Asia,* 21 (4): 36-37.

1159. Mukopadhya, B., 1971, Planning for orthopedically and neurologically handicapped. *The Journal of Rehabilitation in Asia,* 12 (4): 11-14.

1160. Mukundan, P., 1981, Spurt in poliomyelitis in Madras. *Journal of Indian Academy of Pediatrics,* 18 : 539-554.

1161. Nachinolcar, U.G., and Vaid, M.K., 1985, Functional evaluation of orthopedically disabled and handicapped. *The Journal of*

Rehabilitation in Asia, 26 (2): 9-25.

1162. Nair, U.N., and Menon, P.B.M., 1984, Pressure effects following orthotic and prosthetic fitment: A thermo gRaohic profile. *The Journal of Rehabilitation in Asia,* 25 (1): 67-69.

1163. Nanda, A.N., and Rout, S.N., 1989, Prosthetic management of congenital juvenile below elbow amputee, partial hemimelia right limb, *Indian Journal of Disability and Rehabilitation,* 3 (1): 41-46.

1164. Nandanwar, S.A., 1979, Improvised lively wrist driven splint. *The Journal of Rehabilitation in Asia,* 20 (2): 22-23.

1165. Natarajan, K., Joshi, J.B., and Yadav, B.P., 1968, Muscle recovery in the lower limbs in poliomyelitis. *Indian Journal of Pediatrics,* 35 (243): 173-179.

1166. Nimbkar, K., 1960, The employment potential of the physically handicapped. *The Indian Journal of Social Work,* 21 (4): 94-97.

1167. Nimbkar, K.V., 1979, Compulsory education and the crippled child. *The Journal of Rehabilitation in Asia,* 20 (1): 4-8.

1168. Pandey, S., Alam, B., Jha, S.S., Agarwal, S.C., and Pandey, G., 1977, A critical analysis of 837 orthopaedically crippled children attending G N Home for Handicapped Children and Artificial Limb Centre, Ranchi, India. *The Journal of Rehabilitation in Asia,* 18 (1): 18-19.

1169. Pandey, S., Alam, B., Jha, S.S., Agarwal, S.C., and Pandey, Y., 1979, Polioparalysis: A critical review. *The Journal of Rehabilitation in Asia,* 20 (1): 21-27.

1170. Pandey, S., Jha, S.S., Agrawal, S.C., and Pandey, Y., 1976, A simple tarsopronator abduction club foot boot. *The Journal of Rehabilitation in Asia,* 17 (2): 27-28.

1171. Parthasarathy, N.R., 1981, Early detection of physically handicapped cases: Importance of statistical treatment of the problem. *The Journal of Rehabilitation in Asia,* 22 (2): 37-43.

1172. Piplani, C.L., and Mathur, B.P., 1985, Partial loss of the foot. *The Journal of Rehabilitation in Asia,* 26 (2): 29-35.

1173. Prakash, O., and Prakash, R.,1989, Social rehabilitation of hip fracture patients. *Indian Journal of Disability and Rehabilitation,* 3 (2): 61-68.

1174. Prasad. R., Mukherjee, A., and Verma, S.K., 1971, Personality problems of amputees. *The Journal of Rehabilitation in Asia,* 12 (3): 19-21.

1175. Punatar, B., and Patel, D.A., 1977, Pattern of residual paralysis in poliomyelitis. *Indian Journal of Orthopedics,* 11 p 174.

1176. Qadri, S.A., 1960, Assessment of the need in the present set up: Services to the physically handicapped. *The Indian Journal of Social Work,* 20 (4): 97-102.

1177. Ramar, S., 1988, Three tier system for locomotor handicapped. *Indian Journal of Disability and Rehabilitation,* 2 p 63-66.

1178. Rashid, F., 1986, Community oriented physiotheRaoy for polio affected children. *The Journal of Rehabilitation in Asia,* 27 (1): 20-22.

1179. Ravindranath, K.V., and Karunanidhi, S., 1983, Job involvement among the physically disabled. *Journal of Psychological Researches,* 27 (1): 54-57.

1180. Roy, S.C., 1947, Education and rehabilitation of the physically handicapped. *The Indian Journal of Social Work,* 8 (3): 239-247.

1181. Sachdeva, K.C., and Gupta, A.L., 1972, Polio paralysis: Clinical observations and management. *The Journal of Rehabilitation in Asia,* 13 (4): 7-11.

1182. Sahasrabudhe, B.G., and Sancheti, K.H., 1987, Accesibility barriers of orthopedically disabled. *The Journal of Rehabilitation in Asia,* 28 (1): 10-13.

1183. Sahasrabudhe, B.G., and Sancheti, K.H., 1987, A study of life style of orthopedically disabled. *The Journal of Rehabilitation in Asia,* 28 (3): 5-11.

1184. Saksena, R.N., 1962, The physically handicapped in Kanpur. *Journal of Social Sciences,* 3 (1): 1-46.

1185. Samy, A., 1980, Role sheltered workshop in the rehabilitation of the physically handicapped. *The Journal of Rehabilitation in Asia,* 21 (2): 28-31.

1186. Sancheti, K.H., and Sahasrabudhe, B.G., 1979, Rehabilitation of orthopedically handicapped children: Role of medical practitioners in India. *The Journal of Rehabilitation in Asia,* 20 (2): 4-10.

1187. Shanmugasundaram, T.K., and Ramar, S., 1980, Modified postural reduction in spinal fractures with spinal cord injury. *The Journal of Rehabilitation in Asia,* 21 (4): 27-29.

1188. Sharma V.P., Agarwal A.K., Mishra, V.S., and Singhal, A.K.., 1990, A clinical study of upper limb amputees. *Indian Journal of Physical Medicine and Rehabilitation,* 3 (1): 33-36.

1189. Sharma, C.N., Rege, P.V., Athani, B.D., and Ramadas, G., 1992, Analysis of conventional wheel chair. *Indian Journal of Disablity and Rehabilitation,* 6 (1): 25-32.

1190. Sharma, K.C., 1974, Psychiatric aspects of phantom limb and phantom pain phenomenon. *The Journal of Rehabilitation in*

Asia, 15 (4): 22-27.

1191. Sharma, R.K., 1976, Lively splint for radial nerve palsy. *The Journal of Rehabilitation in Asia,* 17 (3): 14-15.

1192. Sharma, R.K., 1977, Wiresplint thenar paralysis. *The Journal of Rehabilitation in Asia,* 18 (3): 14-15.

1193. Sharma, R.K., 1980, Wire splint intrinsic paralysis. *The Journal of Rehabilitation in Asia,* 21 (2): 22-23.

1194. Sharma, R.K., and Yadav, B.P., 1976, Appraisal of treatment of Bells palsy. *The Journal of Rehabilitation in Asia,* 17 (4): 11-16.

1195. Siddiqui, H.D., Awasthi, S.P., and Saifi, A.A.,, 1980, Use of ultrasonic theRaoy in musculoskeletal dysfunction. *The Journal of Rehabilitation in Asia,* 21 (3): 24-28.

1196. Sindva, D., 1991, Job satisfaction and future goals of physically handicapped employees. *Perspectives in Social Work,* 6 (2): 34-35.

1197. Singh, R.P., 1978, Role of rehabilitation in skeletal injuries. *The Journal of Rehabilitation in Asia,* 19 (4): 18-21.

1198. Singh, S.B., Nigam, A., and Nigam, D., 1980, Neuroticism and its different components in physically handicapped. *The Journal of Rehabilitation in Asia,* 21 (2): 24-27.

1199. Srinivasan, T.M., 1978, Electronic below elbow prosthesis for hand prehension. *The Journal of Rehabilitation in Asia,* 19 (1): 4-7.

1200. Srivastava, M., and Anand, R C., 1985, A guide to hospital managers for planning of a hydrotherapy department. *The Journal of Rehabilitation in Asia,* 26 (1): 32-38.

1201. Srivastava, P.N., and Yadav, B.P., 1973, Disorders of gait. *The Journal of Rehabilitation in Asia,* 14 : 20-22.

1202. Srivastava, P.N., 1973, Physiothereupetic management of patients on continuous traction. *The Journal of Rehabilitation in Asia,* 14 (4): 14-15.

1203. Srivastava, P.N., 1974, Physiothereupetic management of a case following patellectomy. *The Journal of Rehabilitation in Asia,* 15 (3): 22-24.

1204. Srivastava, R.C., and Gupta, K.C., 1987, Ultrasonic therapy for painful heel syndrome. *The Journal of Rehabilitation in Asia,* 28 (2): 9-10.

1205. Sunder, S., Janarthanam, A., Ravindranath, L., Jannardhanam, K., and Mangaiyar, K.G., 1989, Case history: Vocational rehabilitation using low cost occupational aids in upper limb prosthesis. *Indian Journal of Disability and Rehabilitation,* 3 (2):

69-72.

1206. Verma, M., 1961, A socio-economic survey of 500 families of the physically handicapped in Kanpur. *The Indian Journal of Social Work,* 21 (4): 447-450.

1207. Verma, S.K., Punj, P., and Kumar, A., 1985, Physio-occupational therapy in management of cervical spondylosis. *The Journal of Rehabilitation in Asia,* 26 (1): 17-22.

1208. Yelurkar, S.K., and Muzumdar, R.D., 1985, Prevalence of physically handicapped in a village and its relation to some of the host factors. *The Journal of Rehabilitation in Asia,* 26 (1): 23-31.

Speech and Hearing Handicap

1209. Abrol, B.M., Dasgupta, G., Pillai, P., and Natu, S.,1972, Rural survey for ENT and speech and hearing defects at village Chhatera. *The Journal of Rehabilitation in Asia,* 13 (2): 24-26.

1210. Abrol, B.M., Raghavan, M.V., 1977, Speech and hearing survey at village Samalkha. *The Journal of Rehabilitation in Asia,* 18 (3): 7-10.

1211. Abrol, B.M., Vagrecha, Y.S., and Saxena, K., 1973, Assessment of intelligence in the patient population having impairment of hearing. *Indian Journal of Mental Retardation,* 6 (2): 75-80.

1212. Abrol, B.M., and Raghavan, M.B., 1978, Fundamental principles in prescribing and fitting of hearing aids in children. *The Journal of Rehabilitation in Asia,* 19 (1): 10-15.

1213. Amesur, C.A., 1952, Rehabilitation of the accoustically handicapped. *Indian Journal of Otolaryngology,* 4 (4): 127-150.

1214. Amesur, C.A., 1961, The modern approaches to deafness. *The Indian Journal of Social Work,* 22 (3): 173-178.

1215. Amin, D.L., 1946, Differences among the deaf and hearing children. *Indian Journal of Psychology,* 21 (1&4): 91-91.

1216. Anand, C.S., and Kishore, K.S., 1974, A new speech discrimination test for children. *The Journal of Rehabilitation in Asia,* 15 (4): 13-16.

1217. Awasthi, S.M., 1981, Jobs for the deaf. *Social Welfare,* 28 (6&7): 16.

1218. Banerjee, S.N., 1957, Employment for the deaf. *Social Welfare,* 3 (12): 3-5.

1219. Basavaraj, V., Menon, N., and Kacker, S.K., 1990, Analysis of voice variation of hearing impaired children belonging to the different Kostic groups. *Indian Journal of Disability and*

Rehabilitation, 4 (2): 1-14.

1220. Belvi, N., 1981, Integration of hearing impaired children into regular school. *Perspectives in Social Work,* 4 (1): 39-41.

1221. Bharadwaj, A., Raghunathan, M., and Mehra, Y.N., 1990, Differential limen for frequency, (DLF) in cochlear impaired listeners. *Indian Journal of Disability and Rehabilitation,* 4 (2): 15-30.

1222. Bharadwaj, A., and Raghunathan, M., 1992, Speech disorders in children. *Indian Journal of Pediatrics,* 59 (5): 615-618.

1223. Bharatraj, J., 1970, The role of clinical psychologist in speech and hearing clinic. *Journal of All India Institute for Speech and Hearing,* 1 : 2.

1224. Bhattacharjee, K., 1936, A short sketch of psychological effect of deafness and its possible means of alleviation. *Indian Journal of Psychology,* 11 : 66-70.

1225. Cama, K.H., 1941, Some recent approaches to speech pathology, speech rehabilitation. *The Indian Journal of Social Work,* 1 (4): 501-514.

1226. Cama, K.H., 1942, Remedial work with speech defectives. *Indian Journal of Psychology,* 17 : 25-34.

1227. Chaddha, N.K., and Gulati, G., 1988, ESP in normal and deaf students: An empirical study. *Disabilities and Impairments,* 2 (1): 1-8.

1228. Chakrabarti, P.K., and Kundu, R., 1986, Language development in low SES children. *Social Change,* 16 (1): 34-37.

1229. Chatterjee, A.K., and Das, S.A.S., 1965, A clinical study of speech difficulties. *Indian Journal of Psychology,* 40 (2): 86-101.

1230. Chattopadhyay, P.K., and Palit, A., 1982, Arousal in handicapped children: A study with deaf and dumb subjects. *Child Psychiatry Quarterly,* 15 (4): 133-135.

1231. D'Sa, N., 1971, The deaf in the 70's. *The Journal of Rehabilitation in Asia,* 12 (1): 5-6.

1232. Das, N., 1954, A comparative study of some mental abilities of deaf mutes and normal children. *Deaf in India,* 6 (3): 1-29.

1233. Das, S.S., 1965, A clinical study of speech difficulties. *Indian Journal of Psychiatry,* 7 (2).

1234. Deka, R.C., Deka, D., Kacker, S.K., and Tandon, D.A., 1986 Auditory brain stem evoked response in risk children. *Indian Journal of Pediatrics,* 53 (4): 651-656.

1235. Deka, R.C., Deka, D., and Kacker, S.K., 1986, Maturation of cochlea, auditory nerve and brain stem as observed by auditory evoked potentials in human infants. *Indian Journal of Otolaryngology,* 38 : 14-17.

1236. Dharitri, I., and Udia, J., 1979, Development of conversation in deaf and dumb children. *Journal of Psychological Researches,* 23 (3): 135-140.

1237. Dutta, P., Mukerjee, A., Verma, S.K., Sanwariya, S., and Singh, N., 1977 Speech recovery in stroke aphasia. *The Journal of Rehabilitation in Asia,* 18 (4): 10-13.

1238. Fazlulla, K.M., 1977, Socio-economic problems of the communicatively handicapped in India. *Journal of All India Institute for Speech and Hearing,* 8 (1): 106-109.

1239. Gargye, A.K., and Dutta, D.V., 1959, Nerve deafness following chloromycetin therapy. *Indian Journal of Pediatrics,* 26 (138): 265-266.

1240. Gupta, R.L., 1965, The problem of deafness in children. *Indian Journal of Pediatrics,* 32 (209): 189-193.

1241. John, K.D., 1965, The hearing defective child in India. *The Journal of Rehabilitation in Asia,* 6 : 1-2.

1242. Kacker, S.K., Basavaraj, V., and Thapar, A., 1989, A study of the prevalence of hearing impairment in the frame work of Kostic Classification System. *Indian Journal of Disability and Rehabilitation,* 3 (2): 1-12.

1243. Kalra, K., Lumba, M., Lal, M., and Dayal, R.S., 1975, Defective articulation in children. *Indian Journal of Pediatrics,* 42 (332): 257-263.

1244. Kalra, K., Sukhiany, A.M., Misra, V.C., and Dayal, R.S., 1975, A clinical analysis of speech defects in children. *Indian Journal of Pediatrics,* 42 (330): 200-208.

1245. Kapur, Y.P., 1963, The hard of hearing child. *Indian Journal of Child Health,* 12 (11): 713-722.

1246. Kapur, Y.P., 1966, Hearing in Indian children. *Indian Journal of Medical Research,* 54 (8) 777-790.

1247. Kashyap, L.D., 1986, The family's adjustment to their hearing impaired child. *The Indian Journal of Social Work,* 47 (1): 31-37.

1248. Kawalgikar, R., 1953, Education and employment of blind and deafmute children. *The Indian Journal of Social Work,* 14 (2): 160-167.

1249. Khan, E., 1953, Care and treatment of deafness. *The Indian Journal of Social Work,* 8 : 4.

1250. Khan, E., 1953, Care and education of deaf children. *The Indian Journal of Social Work,* 13 (4): 237-249.

1251. Khan, E., 1962, Educational problems of the partially deaf. *Social Welfare,* 9 (8): 23-24.

1252. Kharbanda, S., 1981, An enlightened firm for the deaf employees. *Social Welfare,* 28 (6&7): 18.

1253. Kothiyal, K., Mohan, D., and Sahay, K.B., 1986, Rehabilitation aids for communication disabled: Present status of technology in India and future directions. *The Journal of Rehabilitation in Asia,* 27 (2): 5-13.

1254. Kulkarni, S.R., 1974, Development of speech and hearing in Kholapur. *The Journal of Rehabilitation in Asia,* 15 (1): 30-32.

1255. Kumar, S., 1987, Early identification of hearing loss in children, Editorial, *Hearing Aid Journal,* 5 (3): 69-70.

1256. Kumar, S., 1989, Effect of change of earphone on electro acoustic characteristics of a hearing aid. *Indian Journal of Disability and Rehabilitation,* 3 (1): 25-32.

1257. Mahendru, R.K., Srivastava, R.N., and Sharma, D., 1978, Deafness and mental ill-health: A comparative study of deaf and non deaf psychiatric patients. *Indian Journal of Psychiatry,* 20 (2): 148-154.

1258. Majumdar, K., 1963, A study of the personality adjustment of Bangalee deaf and dumb pupils. *Indian Journal of Psychology,* 38 (2): 69-73.

1259. Meena, R., and Mann, S.B.S., 1992, Evaluation of a deaf child. *Indian Journal of Pediatrics,* 59 (5): 609-614.

1260. Mehta, I.B., 1966, The problem of deaf children in India. *The Journal of Rehabilitation in Asia,* 7 : 33.

1261. Mehta, I.B., 1973, The deaf in India. *The Journal of Rehabilitation in Asia,* 14 (2): 25-26.

1262. Menon, N., Basavaraj, V., and Kacker, S.K., 1989, Evaluating the applicability of the Kostic Articulation Test: Applicabilities of the screening test to hearing impaired children,Section 1, *Indian Journal of Disability and Rehabilitation,* 3 (2): 13-20.

1263. Miglani, N., Chahar, C.K., and Gupta, B.D., 1978, Hearing disorders in childhood. *Indian Journal of Pediatrics,* 45 (369): 328-336.

1264. Nagaraja, M.N., 1987, Utility of the hearing aid in deaf children: Parent view. *Hearing Aid Journal,* 5 (3): 88-92.

1265. Nagaraja, M.N., and Shivashankar, N., 1981, General principles of speech and language training with congenital deaf children. *The Journal of Rehabilitation in Asia,* 22 (4): 15-20.

1266. Nigam, J.C., Mehta, B.S., and Abrol, B.M., 1973, Dysphonia: A study of 44 cases. *The Journal of Rehabilitation in Asia,* 14 (1): 21-24.

1267. Nigam, R., 1987, Rehabilitation of aurally handicapped through speech reading. *Hearing Aid Journal,* 5 (2): 53-57.

1268. Pandit, N., 1976, Plans for the implementation of total communication. *The Journal of Rehabilitation in Asia,* 17 (3): 18-21.

1269. Pandit, R., Srinivas, P.S., and Abrol, B.M., 1978, Speech thereupetics for patients with cleft lip and palate. *The Journal of Rehabilitation in Asia,* 19 (4): 11-15.

1270. Pavri, R.R., 1986, The disabled: Deaf. *The Journal of Rehabilitation in Asia,* 27 (3): 13-17.

1271. Pershad, D., Gudi, S.P., and Arora, M.M.L., 1981, Effect of hearing aid on the development of IQ in deaf children. *Child Psychiatry Quarterly,* 14 (2): 55-57.

1272. Ramanjaneyulu, P., and Chandrasekhar, S.S., 1976, Stammering and stuttering. *The Journal of Rehabilitation in Asia,* 17 (1): 13-14.

1273. Ramanjaneyulu, P., and Chandrasekhar, S.S., 1979, Age, eustachian tube function and incidence of conductive hearing loss. *Journal of All India Institute for Speech and Hearing,* 8 (1): 91-95.

1274. Rao, E.M., Mukundan, G., and Kant, A., 1990, Mobilising rural workers in rehabilitation of the speech and hearing handicapped. *Indian Journal of Disability and Rehabilitation,* 4 (1): 45-54.

1275. Ravishanker, K.C., 1987, Speech intelligibility of the hearing impaired: Preliminary results. *Hearing Aid Journal,* 5 (3): 71-76.

1276. Roy, R., and Bhattacharya, R., 1988, Job placement of the deaf vis-a-vis AYJNIHH. *Indian Journal of Disability and Rehabilitation,* 2 : 67-78.

1277. Sahasi, G., 1989, Behaviour problems associated with hearing impairment in children. *Child Psychiatry Quarterly,* 22 (4): 129-132.

1278. Saini, S., 1981. Policy and planning for the deaf. *Indian Journal of Public Administration,* 27 (3): 771.

1279. Samuel, J.D., and Pandalay, S.P.C., 1978, A new speech discrimination test in Tamil. *The Journal of Rehabilitation in Asia,* 19 (2): 4-12.

1280. Sharma, R.S., 1981, Psychological problems of the deaf. *Social Welfare,* 28 (6&7): 15.

1281. Singh, G., and Bagchi, S.C., 1973, A psychosocial assessment of deafmutes. *Indian Journal of Public Health,* 17 (2): 73-76.

1282. Srinivasan, T., 1988, A study of divergent thinking and scholastic achievement of dumb and deaf students. *Child Psychiatry Quarterly,* 21 (3): 109-119.

1283. Srivastava, A.K., 1986, Lalling: A study of speech pathology with special reference to contribution of linguistics. *DEI Research Journal of Education and Psychology,* 4 (1): 29-33.

1284. Teja, J.S., Malhotra, H.K., and Verma, S.K., 1972, The child with speech problem. *Indian Journal of Psychiatry,* 14 (14): 207-211.

1285. Upadhyaya, S., Moudgil, V.K., and Murthy, H.N., 1968, Treatment of stuttering. *Transactions of All India Institute for Mental Health,* 8 : 15-20.

1286. Vasudeva, R., Basavaraj, V., and Kacker, S.K., 1989, Evaluation of the applicability of Kostic Articulation Test: Reliability of the scoring system of the "global test", section 11, *Indian Journal of Disability and Rehabilitation,* 3 (2): 21-30.

1287. Victor, P., 1988, The bridges to success in the management of young deaf children: A model. *Indian Journal of Disability and Rehabilitation,* 2 : 95-106.

Visual Impairment

1288. Agarwal, R., and Singh, M.P., 1988, Primary and recency effects among the blind. *Journal of Psychological Researches,* 32 (1&2): 26-30.

1289. Ahuja, S.C., 1972, The administrative setup in the centre and the states relating to the service for the rehabilitation of the blind and how it can be improved. *The Journal of Rehabilitation in Asia,* 13 (2): 13-15.

1290. Bansal, R.K., Jain, I.S., Kohli, T.K., and Bansal, P.C., 1980, Psychological factors associated with visual impairment. *Indian Journal of Psychiatry,* 22 (2): 173-175.

1291. Basu, A., 1986, The disabled: Blind. *The Journal of Rehabilitation in Asia,* 27 (2): 13.

1292. Basu, A., 1988, Literature for the visually handicapped: An overview. *Disabilities and Impairments,* 2 (2): 168-173.

1293. Chattopadhyay, P.K., and Palit, A., 1982, Arousal in handicapped children: A study with blind subjects. *Child Psychiatry Quarterly,* 15 (4): 131-133.

1294. Dag, G., 1988, Psychosocial profiles of blind adolescent girls. *Indian Journal of Disability and Rehabilitation,* 2 : 1-16.

1295. Desai, H.J.M., 1981, Rehabilitation of the blind in India. *The Indian Journal of Social Work,* 19 (3): 189.

1296. Halder, R.M., 1941, Sight-saving classes in the regular school system as a measure for the prevention of blindness. *The Indian Journal of Social Work,* 2 (4): 515-526.

1297. Halder, R.M., 1941, Social life of the blind. *The Indian Journal of Social Work,* 2 (3): 291-299.

1298. Jain, V.C., and Prasad, B.G., 1968, A socio morbid study of blind school children. *Indian Journal of Pediatrics,* 35 (243): 180-182.

1299. Joshi, I.S., 1981, Aids and appliances for the blind. *The Journal of Rehabilitation in Asia,* 22 (2): 18-21.

1300. Jussawala, K.N.K., 1953, Blind children and their rehabilitation. *The Indian Journal of Social Work,* 13 (4): 257-269.

1301. Jussawala, K.N.K., 1958, The problem of the blind in India. *The Indian Journal of Social Work,* 19 (3): 189-196.

1302. Jussawala, K.N.K., 1958, The preschool blind child. *The Indian Journal of Social Work,* 19 (2): 119-125.

1303. Kitchlu, T.N., 1980, Problems of the newly blind in India. *The Journal of Rehabilitation in Asia,* 21, (3): 17-23.

1304. Kundu, R., Sanyal, N., and Kundu, M., 1984, A comparative study of the visually impaired and sighted persons: Some suggestions for their effective rehabilitation. *The Journal of Rehabilitation in Asia,* 25 (2): 4-9.

1305. Kundu, R., Sanyal, N., and Kundu, M., 1984, A comparative study of the visually impaired and sighted persons. *The Journal of Rehabilitation in Asia,* 25 (3): 34-38.

1306. Mathur, M.L., Choksi, Y.J., and Singh, T.B., 1989, Involvement of parents and family members in rehabilitation of rural blind of Saharanpur District. *Indian Journal of Disability and Rehabilitation,* 3 (2): 45-60.

1307. Mehrotra, K.K., 1979, The blind and their assessment of intelligence. *The Journal of Rehabilitation in Asia,* 20 (3): 8-13.

1308. Mohan, M., 1973, Rehabilitation of the blind. *The Journal of Rehabilitation in Asia,* 14 (4): 25-26.

1309. Mutahaiah, N., 1989, A child with residual vision. *Indian Journal of Disability and Rehabilitation,* 3 (1): 33-40.

1310. Parthasarathy, N.R., and Gupta, C.K., 1962, Influence of some of the socio-economic factors on the prevalence of trachoma. *The Indian Journal of Social Work,* 23 (1): 127-130.

1311. Prasad, L., 1961, Employing the blind in open industry. *The Indian Journal of Social Work,* 21 (4): 403-416.

1312. Prasad, L., 1962, Teachers of the blind in India. *The Indian Journal of Social Work,* 23 (1): 83-98

1313. Routh, T.A., 1962, Psychotherapy as used in a rehabilitation centre for the blind. *The Indian Journal of Social Work,* 23 (2): 173-178.

1314. Roy, S.C., 1943, Vocational guidance of the blind. *The Indian Journal of Social Work,* 4 (4): 213-220.

1315. Roy, S.C., 1946, The blind: Social liabilities or social assets? Part I. *The Indian Journal of Social Work,* 7 (3): 197-203.

1316. Roy, S.C., 1947, The blind: Social liabilities or social assets? Part II. *The Indian Journal of Social Work,* 8 (2): 118-122.

1317. Seth, R.K., 1988, Corneal graftings and eye donations for rehabilitation of visually handicapped. *Indian Journal of Disability and Rehabilitation,* 2 : 85-90.

1318. Sethuraman, S., 1979, A study of the blind workers in a sheltered workshop. *The Journal of Rehabilitation in Asia,* 20 (2): 11-13.

1319. Shastri, A.S.I., 1977, Psychosocial aspects of blindness: Prevention and rehabilitation. *The Journal of Rehabilitation in Asia,* 18 (4) 43-45.

1320. Singh, T.B., 1984, A study of locus of control of visually handicapped persons. *Psychological Studies,* 29 (1): 93-95.

1321. Singh, T.B., and Kainthola, S.D., 1988, WISC-R verbal as a short scale IQ measure for assessment of visually handicapped children: Initial tryouts. *Indian Journal of Disability and Rehabilitation,* 2: 79-94.

1322. Theodore, S., 1978, Self-employment for the blind: A Tiruchi experiment. *The Journal of Rehabilitation in Asia,* 19 (1): 8-9.

1323. Tole, A.P., 1986, Rexine tailoring work as a vocation for the blind. *The Journal of Rehabilitation in Asia,* 27 (3): 1-6.

1324. Verma, P.L., 1971, Probe into the adjustment problem of the blind. *The Indian Journal of Social Work,* 32 (1): 53-62.

1325. Verma, P.L., 1971, Rehabilitation opportunities for the blind in India. *The Indian Journal of Social Work,* 31 (4): 439-447.

1326. Vyas, R.T., 1972, The Royal Commonwealth Society for the Blind, RCSB, declares war on blindness. *The Journal of Rehabilitation in Asia,* 13 (1): 13-14.

Cerebral Palsy

1327. Apte, S.R., 1991, Introduction to 'Cerebral Palsy Group Project' at the BM Institute of Mental Health, Ahmedabad. *Mental Health*

Review, 5 (2): 25-31.

1328. Ashok, P.P., Radhakrishnan, K., Sridharan, R., and Monsa, M.E., 1985, Infantile haemipligia: Clinical EEG and computerised tomography study. *Indian Journal of Pediatrics,* 53 (414): 47-52.

1329. Bassa, D.M., 1966, Some observations on prognosis in cerebral palsy. *Indian Journal of Psychiatry,* 8 (1): 109-113.

1330. Basu, B., 1967, Cerebral palsy in childhood. *Journal of Indian Medical Association,* 49 : 477-482.

1331. Basu, S.N., and Dutta, D. 1977, Non-traumatic paraplegia of upper motor neurone origin in children. *Indian Journal of Pediatrics,* 44 (357): 215-219.

1332. Basu, S.N., and Dutta, D., 1979 Acquired hemiplegia in infancy and childhood. *Indian Journal of Pediatrics,* 46 (379): 274-278.

1333. Datey, K.K., 1979, Hemiplegia in cardiac patients. *The Journal of Rehabilitation in Asia,* 20 (2): 20-21.

1334. Garg, B.K., and Srivastava J.R., 1965, Cerebral palsy: A clinical study of 124 cases with a review. *Indian Pediatrics,* 2 (6): 195-208.

1335. Krishnawamy, P., 1977, Severe and pervasive language defects in educable cerebral palsy children. *The Journal of Rehabilitation in Asia,* 18 (3): 31-32.

1336. Kumar, L.R., Bassi, U., and Patiala, H.S., 1967, Cerebral palsy: Correlation of oneumoencephlography with the clinical picture. *Indian Pediatrics,* 4 (3): 117-124.

1337. Kumar, R.P., 1977, A method of premade dorsal functioning cockup splint for hemiplegics and Volkman's Ischemic contractures. *The Journal of Rehabilitation in Asia,* 18 (4): 18-20.

1338. Makhani, J.S., 1972, Disability of dribbling of saliva in cerebral palsy. *The Journal of Rehabilitation in Asia,* 13 (3): 9-13.

1339. Makhani, J.S., 1973, Management of drooling in cerebral palsy. *The Journal of Rehabilitation in Asia,* 14 (4): 16-19.

1340. Makhani, J.S., 1974, Dribbling of saliva in children with cerebral palsy and its management. *Indian Journal of Pediatrics,* 41 (319): 272-277.

1341. Manchanda, S.S., 1963, Cerebral palsy: A review of 275 cases. *Indian Journal of Child Health,* 12 (1): 1-11.

1342. Mukherjee, A., Bole, S.V., and Verma, S.K., 1971, Cerebral palsy in children: A report of 50 cases. *Indian Journal of Pediatrics,* 38 (279): 219-222.

1343. Nair, K.K., and Virmani, V., 1973, Speech and language disturbances in hemiplegics. *Indian Journal of Medical Research,* 61 (9): 1395-1403.

1344. Rao W.G.R., 1987, Psychological, behavioural and social adjustment in adolescent cerebral palsy. *The Journal of Rehabilitation in Asia,* 28 (3): 12-17.

1345. Sharma, K.C., 1969, Delay and imbalance in milestones as diagnostic indicators for cerebral palsy. *Indian Pediatrics,* 6 : 675.

1346. Sharma, K.C., and Koshy, S., 1972, Psychological impact of cerebral palsy on patients and on their parents. *The Journal of Rehabilitation in Asia,* 13 (4): 27-32.

1347. Sheth, S.S., Karande, S.C., Lahire, K., Jain, M.K., and Shah, M.D., 1990, Hyperlipidernia with infantile hemiplegia *Indian Pediatrics,* 27 (10): 1111-1114.

1348. Singhi, P.D., 1988 Cerebral palsy: Approach and principles of management. *Indian Pediatrics,* 25, (3): 282-287.

1349. Singhi, P.D., 1988, Counselling the parents of a child with cerebral palsy. *Indian Pediatrics,* 25 (4): 368-370.

1350. Solanky, N., Kulkarni, J.S., Kulkarni, S.K., and Makhani, J.S., 1974, Cerebral palsy in children. *The Journal of Rehabilitation in Asia,* 15 (4): 28-34.

1351. Sudrania, S.P., Sharma, S.K., and Singhvi, S.C., 1973, Cerebral palsy: A review. *Indian Journal of Pediatrics,* 40 (309): 371-376.

1352. Udani, P.M., 1963, Cerebral palsy: A study of 100 cases. *Indian Journal of Child Health,* 12 (12): 755-770.

Infantile Autism

1353. Bassa, D.M., 1962, A case of early infantile autism. *Indian Journal of Psychiatry,* 4 (1): 71-76.

1354. Chengappa, S., 1981, Verbal stereotype in autism: A study of expressive language behaviour. *NIMHANS Journal,* 7 (2): 175-180.

1355. Gore, G.B., 1989, Autism: Descriptive case. *NIMHANS Journal,* 7 (1): 83-86.

1356. Kapur, S.O., 1989, Infantile autism: Case studies. *NIMHANS Journal,* 7 (1): 87-90.

1357. Karanth, P., 1981, Pronominal reversal in autism: A note. *NIMHANS Journal,* 7 (2): 181-184.

1358. Khanna, R., and Sood, M., 1991, Autism in tuberous sclerosis. *Indian Journal of Psychiatry,* 33 (2): 149-150.

1359. Krishnamurthy, K., and Joshi, M.R., 1987, A preliminary study of factors associated with infantile autism and their implications. *Child Psychiatry Quarterly,* 20 (3&4): 97-103.

1360. Manjunath, K.R., and Narayanan, H.S., 1981, Cytogenetic investigations in autistic children: A preliminary study on the detection of the fragile X chromosome. *NIMHANS Journal*, 7 (2): 163-168.

1361. Narayanan, H.S., 1978, A report of clinical observations and management in seven cases of childhood autism. *Indian Journal of Psychiatry*, 20 : 93-97.
1362. Rao, A.V., and Sreedhar, K.P., 1975, A case of early infantile autism. *Indian Journal of Psychiatry*, 17 (2): 138-143.
1363. Rao, A.V., and Sreedhar, K.P., 1975, A case of early infantile autism. *Indian Journal of Psychiatry*, 17 (2): 138-143.
1364. Rao, I., 1989, Special educational needs of autistic children. *NIMHANS Journal*, 7 (2): 195-200.
1365. Shivashankar, N., and Satishchandra, P., 1989, Auditory brainstem responses in autistic children. *NIMHANS Journal*, 7 (2): 159-162.
1366. Srilatha, D.R., and Usha, C.A., 1989, Language theRaoy with autistic children: A case report. *NIMHANS Journal*, 7 (2): 195-200.
1367. Srinath, S., Chowdhury, L, Bhide, A.V., Narayanan, H.S., and Shivprakash., 1989, Descriptive study of infantile autism. *NIMHANS Journal*, 7 (1): 83-86.

Juvenile Delinquency

1368. Agarwal, S.S., Sethi, B.E., Sethi, N., and Gupta, A.K., 1978, Dermatoglyphic and buccal smear studies in juvenile delinquency. *Indian Journal of Psychiatry*, 20 p 52-62.
1369. Amati, B.H., 1984, Juvenile delinquency and habit patterns. *The Indian Journal of Social Work*, 34 (4): 405-408.
1370. Badami, H.D., 1962, Psychological study of some factors in juvenile delinquency. *Education and Psychology Review*, 2 (2): 101-106.
1371. Badami, H.D., 1965, Psychological study of factors in juvenile delinquency. *Research Journal of Philosophy and Social Sciences*, 2 (1): 129-141.
1372. Badami, H.D., 1969, Changing concepts of delinquency. *Vidya*, 12 (1): 154-163.
1373. Banerjee, G.R., 1954, Social case work service and the juvenile delinquent. *The Indian Journal of Social Work*, 15 (1): 22-29.
1374. Banerjee, G.R., 1956, Stealing in children. *The Indian Journal of Social Work*, 16 2 o.
1375. Bhattacharya, C.C., 1958, A psychological approach to the problem

of juvenile vagrancy. *Indian Journal of Psychology,* 33 p 171-176.
1376. Bhaumik, G., and Kundu, R., 1982, Some affective personality qualities of delinquent boys. *Social Defence,* 18 (72): 21-26.
1377. Chatterjee, P., and Gutiorrez, F.R., 1978, Juvenile delinqency trends in India and the United States. *The Indian Journal of Social Work,* 39 (1): 93-101.
1378. Chauhan, N.P., and Dixit, B.M., 1965, The home background of the stages of truancy. *Psychological Studies,* 10 (2): 95-103.
1379. Chouhan, V.L., and Bunker, L.N., 1991, A study of social responsibility and security among the scheduled caste and sceduled tribe juvenile delinquents. *Journal of Personality and Clinical Studies,* 7 (2): 203-206.
1380. De, S.K., 1970, Intelligence and crime. *Educational Review,* 76 (6): 128-1129.
1381. Deol, G., 1990, Juvenile delinquency in India. *Social Change,* 20 (3): 59-70.
1382. Doraiswami, K., 1940, A study of 100 cases of juvenile delinquency in the city of Madras. *The Indian Journal of Social Work,* 1 (1): 48-55.
1383. Gokhale, S.D., 1954, Juvenile delinquency in relation to social influence. *The Indian Journal of Social Work,* 15 (1): 6-11.
1384. Gokhale, S.D., 1982, Juvenile delinquency. *Social Change,* 12 (3): 22-25.
1385. Iyer, D.S., Desousa, A., and Khilanani, D.K., 1969, Delinquency: An analysis of 25 cases. *Child Psychiatry Quarterly,* 2 (3): 13-21.
1386. Jadhav, M.C., 1961, Correctional work for juvenile delinquents. *The Indian Journal of Social Work,* 22 (1): 47-54.
1387. Jaffe, L.D., 1963, Recent research in juvenile delinquency. *The Indian Journal of Social Work,* 24 (2): 106-109.
1388. Jain, V.C., and Prasad, B.G., 1968, A social study of delinquent children. *Indian Journal of Pediatrics,* 35 (246): 331-333.
1389. Jairam, C., 1984, Juvenile delinquency and law. *Social Defence,* 19 (75): 5-10.
1390. Jayashankarappa, B.S., and Rao, D.C.V.P., 1971, A study of some aspects of psychosocial pathology of juvenile delinquency. *Indian Journal of Pediatrics,* 38 (281): 265-271.
1391. Kabbar, S.K., 1989, Personality correlates of institutionalised delinquents. *Indian Psychological Review,* 34 (3&4): 10-16.
1392. Kaliappan, K.V., and Kannappan, P.K., 1984, Effect of behaviour therapy techniques on state and trait anxieties of juvenile delinquents. *Social Defence,* 19 (75): 16-21.

1393. Kaliappan, K.V., and Senthilathiban, K., 1984, Anxiety among delinquents. *Indian Journal of Criminology,* 12 (1): 58-60.

1394. Khan, I.A., Khan, A.A., and Husain, M.M., 1982, An inventory for juvenile delinquency. *Indian Journal of Criminology,* 10 (1): 47-52.

1395. Khan, S.A., Jusain, M.Q., and Irfan, M., 1991, Anxiety and level of aspiration among criminals. *Journal of Personality and Clinical Studies,* 7 (2): 191-194.

1396. Kishore, B., Verma, H.C., and Shah, D.K., 1970, An analysis of 380 criminal mental patients. *Indian Journal of Psychiatry,* 12 (1&2): 117-124.

1397. Kochavara, T.L., 1952, The delinquent child. *The Indian Journal of Social Work,* 13 (3): 168-174.

1398. Kodandaram, P., 1986, Family size and delinquency. *Indian Journal of Psychological Medicine,* 9 (2): 89-90.

1399. Kulkarni, A., 1952, Juvenile delinquency. *The Indian Journal of Social Work,* 12 (4): 450-454.

1400. Kundu, C.L., 1969 Intelligence and tribal delinquency. *Indian Journal of Applied Psychology,* 6 (1): 2-30.

1401. Kundu, R., and Bhaumik, G., 1982, Introversion extraversion and nueroticism: Two outstanding personality correlates of juvenile delinquency boys. *Indian Journal of Criminology,* 10 (1): 37-41.

1402. Leelavathi, K.V., and Murthy, H.N., 1969, Factors affecting rehabilitation of delinquents. *Transactions of All India Institute for Mental Health,* 9 : 75-79.

1403. Majumdar, A., 1961, Vagrancy in West Bengal. *The Indian Journal of Social Work,* 22 (3): 229-232.

1404. Majumdar, A.K., and Roy, A.B., 1962, Latest personality content of juvenile delinquents. *Journal of Psychological Researches,* 6 (1): 4-8.

1405. Manshardt, C., 1940, The Bombay Children Act: Its provision and procedure under the act in the city of Bombay. *The Indian Journal of Social Work,* 1 (1): 31-42.

1406. Marfatia, J.C., 1956 Stealing in children. *The Indian Journal of Social Work,* 16 (3): 9-15

1407. Marfatia, J.C., 1969, Juvenile delinquency. *The Indian Journal of Social Work,* 30 (1): 1-9.

1408. Mehendale, Y.S., 1955, Physical environment and adoloscent crimes. *The Indian Journal of Social Work,* 16 : 146-152.

1409. Mehendale, Y.S., 1955, The adolescent criminal. *The Indian Journal of Social Work,* 16 : 33-39.

1410. Mehendale, Y.S., 1957, Occupational disasters and adolescent crime. *The Indian Journal of Social Work,* 18 : 25-28.

1411. Mehendale, Y.S., 1959, Abuses, imputation and social ostracism as factors in crime causation. *The Indian Journal of Social Work,* 20 (1): 33-38.

1412. Mehendale, Y.S., 1960, The adolescent criminal. *Social Welfare,* 7 (6): 13-16.

1413. Mishra, V.D., 1982, Some personality characteristics of juvenile delinquents. *Social Defence,* 18 (71): 32-36.

1414. Mukerji, N., 1955, Sexual delinquency. *The Indian Journal of Social Work,* 16 : 19-26.

1415. Mukherjee, B.N., 1956, Psychological approach to juvenile delinquency. *The Indian Journal of Social Work,* 17 (1): 12-20.

1416. Mukherjee, K., and Kundu, S., 1961, A study of birth order and family positions of the criminals. *Indian Journal of Psychology,* 36 (3): 127-132.

1417. Murthy, H.N., 1966, Crime and temperament. *Psychological Studies,* 11 (1): 15-22.

1418. Muthayya, B.C, and Baskaran, A.S., 1964, Some factors of juvenile delinquency and sibship position. *Indian Journal of Applied Psychology,* 1 (2): 116-126.

1419. Nath, L., 1940, A study of 35 stealing cases passing through the Bombay Juvenile Court in 1939. *The Indian Journal of Social Work,* 1 (1): 65-72.

1420. Orgel, S.Z., 1968, Delinquency. *Samiksha,* 22 (3): 81-86.

1421. Pagdiwalla, K.D., and Pestonjee, D.M., 1988, A study of need patterns in orphans, delinquents and physically handicapped. *Journal of Personality and Clinical Studies,* 4 (1): 23-30.

1422. Panakal, J.J., 1961, Juvenile delinquency. *The Indian Journal of Social Work,* 22 (3): 263-266.

1423. Panakal, J.J., 1961, Special training of police for prevention of juvenile delinquency. *The Indian Journal of Social Work,* 22 (2): 139-141.

1424. Pathak, S., 1984, The community and the delinquent child. *Agra University Journal of Research,* 11 (2): 7-21.

1425. Pati, G., 1965, Intelligence of the delinquents compared with that of criminals and normal juveniles of Orissa. *Indian Journal of Applied Psychology,* 2 (1): 17-20.

1426. Pati, G., 1966, Pesonaliity pathology of deliquent. *Psychological Studies,* 11 (1): 35-41.

1427. Phatak, P., 1962, Mental health in relation to the delinquent child.

Indian Journal of Public Health, 6 (2): 87-89.

428. Ramana, K.V., 1972, Role of subcultures in juvenile delinquency: A critique of three sociological perspective. *The Indian Journal of Social Work,* 33 (2): 125-132.

1429. Ravindranath, K.V., and David, B., 1982, A comparative study of the intelligence of delinquents and normals. *Indian Journal of Criminology,* 10 (1): 33-36.

1430. Ray, A.B., 1963, A verbal test to identify delinquents. *The Indian Journal of Social Work,* 24 (1): 40-42.

1431. Sabnis, M.S., 1954, Delinquency and preventive corrections. *The Indian Journal of Social Work,* 14 (4): 426-434.

1432. Sandhu, H.S., 1960, Validation of socialisation scale for delinquency scale in India. *The Indian Journal of Social Work,* 21 (2): 155-166.

1433. Sen, A., 1982, Juvenile delinquency and mental health problems. *Social Change,* 12, (4): 13-19.

1434. Sen, J.M., 1937, A study of certain characteristics of delinquent boys. *Indian Journal of Psychology,* 12 p 163.

1435. Shanmugam, T.E., 1948, An analytical study of delinquents. *The Indian Journal of Social Work,* 9 (3): 176-184.

1436. Shariff, I.A., and Sekar, K., 1982, Social predictors in juvenile delinquency. *Indian Journal of Criminology,* 10 (1): 42-46.

1437. Shekar, S., 1981, Delinquency and school. *The Indian Journal of Social Work,* 32 (1): 9-19.

1438. Shukla, K.S., 1977, Adolescent thieves: Family structure. *The Indian Journal of Social Work,* 27 (4): 393-406.

1439. Shukla, K.S., 1982, Delinquency control: The institutional strategy. *The Indian Journal of Social Work,* 43 (3): 283.

1440. Siddiqi, A.H., 1982, Juvenile delinquency in developed and developing countries. *Social Defence,* 18 (69): 18-29.

1441. Sikka, K.D., 1981, Juvenile delinquency and the mass media. *The Indian Journal of Social Work,* 22 (2): 105-112.

1442. Sikka, K.D., 1983, After care programmes for juveniles: Where does it stand today. *The Indian Journal of Social Work,* 44 (2): 157-166.

1443. Singh, A., 1980, A study of the personality and adjustment of female juvenile delinquents. *Child Psychiatry Quarterly,* 13 (2): 52-59.

1444. Singh, A., 1980, Personality of female truants. *Child Psychiatry Quarterly,* 13 (2): 60-66.

1445. Singh, A., and Sharma, S., 1977, The effect of broken home on juvenile delinquency. *Indian Psychological Review,* 15 p 10-14.

1446. Singh, O.P., and Agarwal, P., 1986, Family environment and delinquency. *Indian Journal of Criminology,* 14 (2): 144-151.

1447. Singh, V.P., 1967, Extraversion-neuroticism: Their distribution in criminals. *Indian Journal of Applied Psychology,* 4 (1): 24-27.

1448. Singh, V.P., 1970, The self concept of both criminal male and female: A comparative study. *Psychological Studies,* 15 (2): 101-107.

1449. Sinha, D., and Singh, V.P., 1969, The self concept of criminals. *Psychological Studies,* 13 (2): 118-125.

1450. Sivanandam, C., 1971, A study of frustration reaction in delinquent and non-delinquent children. *The Indian Journal of Social Work,* 32 (2): 151-154.

1451. Srivastava, S., and Selvi, G., 1988, A comparative study of the level of intelligence of deaf and normal children of the ages 9, 10 and 11 years. *Child Psychiatry Quarterly,* 21 (3): 87-108.

1452. Srivastava, V.S., 1960, Delinquency control and probation. *The Indian Journal of Social Work,* 21 (3): 267-270.

1453. Tandon, A.K., 1977, Psychosocial variables in a delinquent group. *Indian Journal of Pediatrics,* 44 (351): 245-252.

1454. Thilagaraj, R., 1983, Parent child relationship and juvenile delinquency. *Social Defence,* 19 (73): 20-26.

1455. Thilagaraj, R., 1985, Level of aspiration of delinquents and non-delinquents: A comparative study. *Indian Journal of Criminology,* 13 (2): 132-138.

1456. Thilagaraj, R., 1987, Goal perception of delinquents and non-delinquents: Comparative study. *Indian Journal of Criminology,* 15 (2): 145-149.

1457. Vijayalakshmi, G., 1988, Suggestability in delinquents and non delinquents. *Child Psychiatry Quarterly,* 21 (1): 7-12.

Learning Disability

1458. Dharitri, R., 1992, Learning disablity: A case report. *Indian Journal of Clinical Psychology,* 19 (2): 82-83.

1459. Khanna, S., 1980, Non intellectual factors in learning diasability. *Indian Journal of Psychiatry,* 22 (3): 256-260.

1460. Sarangi, H., 1989, Learning disabilities: A psychoeducational perspective. *Disabilities and Impairments,* 3 (1): 38-46.

1461. Venkatesan, S., and Vepuri, V.G.D., 1993, Content errors in prearithmetic peroformance of children with specific arithmetic retardation. *Journal of Psychological Researches* 37 (1&2): 46-51

General

1462. Abraham, L., Somasundaram, C.P., and Mathai, K.V., 1973, Social adjustment, social and vocational rehabilitation of persons with convulsive disorders. *The Journal of Rehabilitation in Asia,* 14 (3): 4-9.

1463. Agarwal, A.K., and Sithcley, P., 1978, Gilles de la Tourettes syndrome: A case report. *Indian Journal of Psychiatry,* 20 p 91.

1464. Aiyer, S.R., and Krishnaswamy, S., 1989, Values of handicapped *vis-a-vis* normal adolescents. *Indian Journal of Disability and Rehabilitation,* 3 (1): 1-18.

1465. Badonia, O.P., Dhodapkar V.G., Pohowalla, J.N., and Singh, M., 1968, Intellectual development of school age groups of children. *Indian Journal of Medical Research,* 56 (11): 1651-1662.

1466. Bal, B.K.S., 1966, An interesting case report on Gilles de la Tourette's disease. *Indian Journal of Psychiatry,* 8 : 238.

1467. Bharati, V.V., and Venkataramaiah, S.R., 1988, Anxiety and language function. *Child Psychiatry Quarterly,* 21 (2) 33-42.

1468. Bhargava, S., Garg, O.P., Singh, S., Singh, P., and Lall, K.B., 1988, Prevalence of behaviour problems in Ajmer school children. *Indian Journal of Pediatrics,* 55 (3) 408-415.

1469. Bhasin, M.P., 1989, School maturation: Theoretical and practical approaches. *Journal of Indian Education,* 14 (2): 13-17.

1470. Bhatia, M.S., Singhal, P.K., Dhar, N.K., Nigam, V.R., Malik, S.C., and Mullick, D.N., 1990, Breath holding spells: An analysis of fifty cases. *Indian Pediatrics,* 27, (10): 1073-1079.

1471. Bhattacharya, D.D., and Singh, R., 1971, Operant manipulation of behaviour problem. *Indian Journal of Pediatrics,* 33 (281): 309-312.

1472. Bhattacharya, A.K., and Mandal, J.N., 1967, Battered child syndrome: A review with a report of two siblings. *Indian Pediatrics,* 4 (4): 186-194.

1473. Bhogle, S., Vanaja, J.T., and Lakshmi, P.A., 1986, Aggression and dependency behaviour in pre school children. *Social Change,* 16 (1): 14-19.

1474. Billimora, R.B., 1992, The principle of normalisation: An ideology. *Indian Journal of Disability and Rehabilitation,* 6 (1): 39-44.

1475. Chakrabarty, A., 1962, Gilles de la Tourette's disease. *Indian*

Journal of Psychiatry, 4 (2): 187-189.

1476. Chandra, R.K., 1964, Association of breath holding attacks with anemia and their treatment. *Indian Journal of Pediatrics,* 31 (196): 143-144.

1477. Chandra, R.K., 1965, Association of breath holding attacks with anemia and their treatment. *Indian Pediatrics,* 2 (8): 295-297.

1478. Chatterjee, K.K., and Chaudhury, N.J., 1961, Lipid metabolism in malnutrition in children. *Indian Journal of Pediatrics,* 28 : 195.

1479. Chaturvedi, P.K., Agarwal, A.K., and Gupta, S.C., 1984, Psychological study of inmates of a childrens home with specific reference to their intelligence and aggressive behaviour. *Indian Journal of Psychiatry,* 26 (2): 133-140.

1480. Chaudhuri, S., 1989, Mother based management: Paradigm for holistic health care as a participative model for rural development. *Social Action,* 39 : 255-283.

1481. Chawla, P.L., Sahasi, G., Sundaram, K.R., and Mehta, M., 1982, A study of prevalence and pattern of hyperactive syndrome in primary school children. *Indian Journal of Psychiatry,* 24 (4): 313-322.

1482. Chittibabu, A., 1980, Rural Rehabilitation: Must it remain a theoretical ideal on paper?. *The Journal of Rehabilitation in Asia,* 21 (4): 38-40.

1483. Chopdar, A., 1979, Integrated Child Development Services Scheme,ICDSS,: A new approach to maternal and child health services. *Indian Journal of Pediatrics,* 46 (373): 53-57.

1484. Currimbhoy, Z., 1963, Growth and development in Bombay children. *Indian Journal of Child Health,* 12 (11): 627.

1485. Dattabanik, N.D., 1979, Psychosocial behavioural problems of children during adolescence. *Indian Journal of Pediatrics,* 46 (375): 121-125.

1486. Dattabanik, N.D., Krishna, R., Mane, S.I.S., and Lala, R., 1970, Longitudinal growth pattern of children during pre school age. *Indian Journal of Pediatrics,* 37 : 438.

1487. Dhar, B.N., 1981, Statutory requirements for voluntary organisations. *Social Welfare,* 28 (8): 36.

1488. Gada, M., 1987, A study of prevalence and pattern of attention deficit disorder with pattern of attention deficit disorder with hyperactivity in primary school children. *Indian Journal of Psychiatry,* 29 (2): 113-118.

1489. Gandhi, J.S., 1980, A study of rehabilitation achievement: Comparison between British and Indian studies. *Indian Journal of Mental Retardation,* 13 : 33.

1490. Ganesan, V., and Vijayakumar, S., 1977, The disadvantaged creative child. *The Journal of Rehabilitation in Asia,* 18 (3) 7-10.

1491. George, J., 1988, Science teaching for handicapped. *Indian Journal of Disability and Rehabilitation,* 2 : 11-18.

1492. Gokhale, S.D., 1967, Development in the field of rehabilitation in India. *The Indian Journal of Social Work,* 28 (3): 291-295.

1493. Gulati, P.V., 1978 Criteria for planning and layout of a medical rehabilitation department in a developing country. *The Journal of Rehabilitation in Asia,* 19 (3) 4-11.

1494. Gupta, J.P., 1968, A exploratory study of absenteeism in a school in urban area in New Delhi. *Indian Journal of Pediatrics,* 35 (246): 299-313.

1495. Gupta, P., 1983, Frustration in socially disadvantaged adolescents. *Child Psychiatry Quarterly,* 16 (1): 34-38.

1496. Hurkat, P.C., 1990, New dimensions in the causes and cures in childhood disabilities. *Indian Journal of Disability and Rehabilitation,* 4 (1): 71-74.

1497. Jaganadham, V., 1985, A conceptual essay on the relationship between governmental and non governmental agencies. *Social Action,* 15 (1): 13-16.

1498. Jain, A.M., 1968, Planning and organisation of child health services in rural India:,1, Well Child Care Centre, 2, School Health Service. *Indian Journal of Pediatrics,* 35 (242): 146-155.

1499. Jain, M.L., and Agarwal, D., 1985, Overview of anganwadi centres in an ICDS tribal block. *Indian Journal of Pediatrics,* 52 (415): 151-154.

1500. Keswani, M.H., 1976, Community participation in rehabilitation. *The Journal of Rehabilitation in Asia,* 17 (4): 7-10.

1501. Khatri, A., 1965, Intellectual deficit of orphanaged reared children: A further study. *Indian Journal of Medical Research,* 53 (1): 1040-1051.

1502. Khatri, A., 1965, Differences in goals, interests, intelligence, scholastic performance, etc., of orphanage reared children and family reared children. *Indian Journal of Applied Psychology,* 2: 28-38.

1503. Khosla, S.N., 1963, Childhood obesity: An analysis of 25 cases and a case report of Laurence Moon Biedl syndrome. *Indian Journal of Child Health,* 12 (6): 350-355.

1504. King, P., 1964, Rehabilitation: A community responsibility. *The Nursing Journal of India,* 72 (11): 311-312.

1505. Krishnamurthy, K., and Bhagirati, G.M., 1986, Child mental health services through ICDS. *Child Psychiatry Quarterly,* 19 (1): 26-35.

1506. Krishnaswamy, S., 1987, The demogRaohy of the disabled and the handicapped in India. *The Indian Journal of Social Work,* 48 (1): 83-94.

1507. Kumar, K.M.P., Aninuni, A.C., Menon, P.S.N., Khurana, M.L., Karmarkar, M.G., and Ahuja, M.M.S., 1987, Sexual precocity: Clinical profile and laboratory evaluation. *Indian Journal of Pediatrics,* 54 (6): 897-902.

1508. Kumar, R., 1976, A review of research in child health and nutrition. *The Indian Journal of Social Work,* 37 (2): 171-185.

1509. Kushwaha, K.P., Mathur, G.P., Mathur, S., Singh, Y.D., and Sati, T.R., 1986, Superstitious therapy during illnesses of pre school children. *Indian Pediatrics,* 23 : 163-168.

1510. Malhotra, S., Verma, V.K., Verma, S.K., and Malhotra, A., 1988, Childhood Psychopathology Measurement Schedule, CPMS,: Development and standardisation. *Indian Journal of Pediatrics,* 55 : 325-332.

1511. Malhotra, S., Verma, V.K., and Verma, S.K., 1986, Temperament as determinent of phenomenology of childhood psychiatry disorders. *Indian Journal of Pediatrics,* 97 : 263-276.

1512. Malhotra, S., and Chaturvedi, S.K., 1983, Rutter's multi axial system of classification of childhood psychiatric disorders: Applicability and usefulness. *Child Psychiatry Quarterly,* 16 (2) 76-85.

1513. Malhotra, S., and Chaturvedi, S.K., 1984, Patterns of childhood psychiatric disorders in India. *Indian Journal of Pediatrics,* 51 : 235-240.

1514. Malhotra, S., and Malhotra, A., 1990, Psychological adjustment of physically sick children: Relationship with temperament. *Indian Pediatrics,* 27 (6) 577-584.

1515. Malin, A.J., 1972, Inter-disciplinary coordination and team work. *Indian Journal of Mental Retardation,* 5 (1): 41-43.

1516. Marfatia, J.C., 1945, Fits of psychological origin. *The Indian Journal of Social Work,* 6 (3): 183-191.

1517. Marfatia, J.C., 1953, Children with behaviour problems. *The Indian Journal of Social Work,* 13 (4): 217-224.

1518. Marfatia, J.C., 1958, Cultural and social factors contributing to child's maladjustment. *The Indian Journal of Social Work,* 19 (2): 115-118.

1519. Mathur, M.N.L., 1986, Possibilities of community oriented work by clinical psychologists: Challenges and barriers. *Journal of Personality and Clinical Studies,* 2 (2): 141-145.

1520. Mehta, M., 1991, Pediatricians role in corporal punishment. *Indian Journal of Pediatrics,* 58 (4): 731-732.

1521. Menon, M.S., Gitavani, C., and Saraswati, K., 1978, Rehabilitation of female patients in Government Mental Hospital, Madras. *The Journal of Rehabilitation in Asia,* 19 (2): 20-25.

1522. Menon, S.M., Nagaswami, V., and Thara, R., 1985, Recent trends in rehabilitation research. *Indian Journal of Social Psychiatry,* 1 (1): 30-40.

1523. Menon, S.N., 1987, District Rehabilitation Centre Scheme: A pilot project. *Indian Journal of Disability and Rehabilitation,* 1: 23-25.

1524. Miranda, M.M., 1985, A new perspective in medical social work and its implications for teaching. *The Indian Journal of Social Work,* 45 (4): 442-447.

1525. Misra, R.S., Bhagoliwal, A., Bhalla, J.N., Singh, S.B., and Rohatagi, P., 1980, An exploration study of health and mental status of children. *Child Psychiatry Quarterly,* 13 (1): 18-23.

1526. Mohan, V., Varma, V.K., and Sawhney, B.B., 1976, Intellectual and memory functions in epileptics. *Neurology in India,* 24 : 110.

1527. Mukherjee, S., 1991, Rural health services. *Indian Journal of Pediatrics,* 58 (4): 407-414.

1528. Mukherjee, S., 1991, The girl child in India. *Indian Journal of Pediatrics,* 58 (3): 301-304.

1529. Murthy, R.S., Wig, N.N., and Harding, T.W., 1981, A model for rural psychiatric services: Raipur Rani experience. *Indian Journal of Psychiatry,* 23 : 275.

1530. Narchal, R., and Juneja, M., 1987, Children's drawings as measures of intellectual ability. *Journal of Personality and Clinical Studies,* 3 (1): 39-42.

1531. Nayar, S., Singh, D., Rao, N.P., and Chaudhary, D.P., 1990, Primary school teacher as a primary health care worker. *Indian Journal of Pediatrics,* 57 (1): 77-80.

1532. Nimbkar, K.V., 1976, Vocational rehabilitation and the community, where do we start?. *The Journal of Rehabilitation in Asia,* 17 (3): 8-10

1533. Pakrasi, K., Halder, A., and Basumallik, T., 1973, Bio social characteristics of the mentally disordered: An exploratory study *The Indian Journal of Social Work,* 35 (1): 75-88.

1534. Parikh, R., 1992, Position paper on the use of punishment in the field of teaching children with behaviour disorders. *Indian Journal of Disability and Rehabilitation,* 6 (1): 61-68.

1535. Paul, R., and Manchanda, S.S., 1969, Breath holding attacks: The role of psychological factors and iron therapy. *Indian Journal of Pediatrics,* 36 (259): 271-277.

1536. Prasad, L.S.N., 1958, Adreno genital syndrome in a boy of four years. *Indian Journal of Pediatrics,* 25 p 427.

1537. Prasad, L.S.N., and Webb, J.K.G., 1959, Review of a case of preccocious puberty in a boy of four years. *Indian Journal of Pediatrics,* 26 (137): 215-219.

1538. Puri, R., and Mehta, S., 1988, Preschool teachers,Balsevikas, in service orientation in nutrition and health education: An impact study. *Indian Journal of Pediatrics,* 55 (4): 605-610.

1539. Radhakrishnan, E.P., 1981, Good foundation for meaningful rehabilitation. *Yojana,* 25 (14&15): 26.

1540. Raju, Y.R.R.P., and Venugopal, M., 1986, Levels of scholastic acheivement and severity of emotional problems. *Child Psychiatry Quarterly,* 19 (2&3): 104-107.

1541. Rao S.L., 1993, Cognitive deficits in epilepsy. *NIMHANS Journal,* 11 (1): 11-20.

1542. Rao S.L., Srinath, S., Aroor, S.A., and Kaliaperumal, V.G., 1992, Neuropsychological deficits in children with epilepsy. *NIMHANS Journal,* 10 (1): 85-93.

1543. Rao W.G.R., 1977, Indian Society for the Rehabilitation of the Handicapped. *The Journal of Rehabilitation in Asia,* 18 (3): 19-20.

1544. Rao W.G.R., 1980, Rehabilitation in India. *The Journal of Rehabilitation in Asia,* 21 (1): 3-4.

1545. Ravikanth, A.L., 1990, Information processing models of teaching: An analysis. *Journal of Indian Education,* 15 (5): 19-23.

1546. Ray, C.N., 1990, Implementation of ICDS in eastern Uttar Pradesh. *Social Change,* 20 (3): 71-79.

1547. Sandhu, R.K., and Ghai, O.P., 1968, Study of physical growth of Indian children in Delhi. *Indian Journal of Pediatrics,* 35 : 91.

1548. Satyanand, D., and Singh, M.V., 1967, Ambulatory domiciliary management of mental health problems in India. *Indian Journal of Medical Research,* 55 (4): 785.

1549. Satyavati, K., and Golam, G.R., 1976, Rehabilitation or rehospitalisation. *The Journal of Rehabilitation in Asia,* 17 (4): 17-25.

1550. Sen, A.K., 1980, Problems of rehabilitation. *Indian Journal of Mental Retardation,* 13 (1&2): 28-32.

1551. Shah, N., 1971, The concept of occupational therapy in psychiatry at KEM hospital, Bombay. *The Journal of Rehabilitation in Asia,* 12 (1): 31-33.

1552. Sharma, R.K., and Yadav, E.P., 1978, Hand dynamometer. *The Journal of Rehabilitation in Asia,* 19 (1): 19.

1553. Sharma, V., 1986, Critical assessment of monitoring and evaluation of ICDS programme and profile of suggested indicators in the social components. *The Indian Journal of Social Work,* 47 (3): 303.

1554. Singh, G., 1968, Growth and development of social welfare organisation in Punjab. *The Indian Journal of Social Work,* 28 (4): 453-466.

1555. Singh, M.V., 1971, Mental health in children: Problems of diagnosis and treatment. *Indian Journal of Pediatrics,* 38 (281): 272-275.

1556. Singh, M.V., 1980, Community mental health and Child Guidance Centre. *Child Psychiatry Quarterly,* 13 (4): 94-94.

1557. Singh, M.V., and Sahay, M., 1974, Mental health in children: Education and prevention. *Indian Journal of Pediatrics,* 41 (312): 19-21.

1558. Singh, S.B., Rathi, A.K., Gupta, V., Gupta, K., and Nigam, A., 1979, Personality and IQ of epileptic children. *Child Psychiatry Quarterly,* 12 (3): 73-77.

1559. Singhal, P.K., Bhatia, M.S., Dhar, N.K., and Nigam, V.R., 1987, Habit disorders: Prevalence and etiology. *Indian Pediatrics,* 24 : 475-479.

1560. Singhal, P.K., Bhatia, M.S., Nigam, V.R., and Bohra, N., 1988, Thumb sucking: An analysis of 150 cases. *Indian Pediatrics,* 25 (7): 647-653.

1561. Singhi, S., Broca, J.S., and Mathur, G.M., 1987, Smoking behaviour in rural school boys. *Indian Pediatrics,* 24 (8): 655-659.

1562. Sinha, K.K., 1984, Epilepsy: Social aspects. *Social Change,* 14 (3): 37-40.

1563. Sinha, S.P., 1989, Significance of behaviour modification techniques in classroom setting. *Journal of Indian Education,* 14 (4): 63-67.

1564. Somasundaram, C.P., Mathai, K.V., and Rao, D., 1971, A survey of public knowledge and attitude towards epilepsy and epileptics. *The Journal of Rehabilitation in Asia,* 12 (2): 4-17.

1565. Somasundaram, C.P., and Mathai, K.V., 1972, Attitude of industrial and business concerns towards persons disabled by convulsive disorders: A preliminary study. *The Journal of Rehabilitation in Asia,* 13 (1): 9-12.

1566. Somasundaram, C.P., and Mathai, K.V., 1972, Self evaluation of epileptics and parental attitudes towards epileptic children. *The Journal of Rehabilitation in Asia,* 13 (4): 14-19.

1567. Somen, K.S., 1986, A study of the mental health status on children in orphanages at Bangalore. *The Indian Journal of Social Work,* 47 (2): 137-146.

1568. Srivastava, R.N., 1987, Need for sex education, Editorial, *Indian Pediatrics,* 24 (6): 457-460.

1569. Suman, S.K., 1986, Social work with disturbed school children. *Child Psychiatry Quarterly,* 19 (2&3): 67-78.

1570. Suman, S.K., and Reddy, G.N., 1985, Mental health care delivery to rural areas: An Indian experiment. *Perspectives in Social Work,* 2 (1): 1-8.

1571. Surty, T., 1971, Integrated approach to rehabilitation. *The Journal of Rehabilitation in Asia,* 12 (3): 22-23.

1572. Tanya, D.K., Singhal, P.K., and Dhanan, S., 1988, Superstitions in pediatric illnesses among rural mothers. *Indian Pediatrics,* 25 (5): 447-452.

1573. Thakker, D., 1989, Mental health in school children: Role of teachers. *The Indian Journal of Social Work,* 50 (4): 439-450.

1574. Thakur, G.P., 1987, Industrialisation and mental health. *Social Change,* 17 (4): 79-86.

1575. Thangavar, N., 1986, A study of sex differences on Seguin Form Board Test. *Child Psychiatry Quarterly,* 19 : 4.

1576. Thomas, D., 1978, The principle of normalisation. *Indian Journal of Mental Retardation,* 11 (1): 23-35.

1577. Tomar, B.S., 1980, Superstitions and child health. *Indian Pediatrics,* 17 : 883-885.

1578. Trivedi, J.K., and Sethi, B.B., 1979, Maturational factors and diagnostic break up of patients seeking traditional healing methods. *Indian Journal of Psychiatry,* 21 (3): 240-246.

1579. Tyagi, T.S., 1987, Astrology and mental health. *Journal of Personality and Clinical Studies,* 3 (1): 63-66.

1580. Udani, P.M., 1963, Physical growth in children in different socio-economic and nutritional groups. *Indian Journal of Child Health,* 12 (10): 593.

1581. Udani, R.H., Chottani, S., Arora, S., and Kulkarni, C.S., 1980,

Evaluation of knowledge and efficiency of anganwadi workers. *Indian Journal of Pediatrics,* 47 (387): 289-292.

1582. Uma, H., and Kapur, M., 1982, A study of behaviour problems in preschool children. *NIMHANS Journal,* 8 (1): 69-73.

1583. Upadhyaya, S.K., Agarwal, D.K., Agarwal, K.N., Srivastava, K.B., and Adhikari, S.G., 1988, Brief fasting and cognitive functions in rural school children. *Indian Pediatrics,* 25 (3): 288-289.

1584. Vaidya, R.A., 1982, Diagnostic approach and management of precocious puberty. *Indian Journal of Pediatrics,* 49 : 254-257.

1585. Varma, R.M., 1976, Voluntary organisation's: The changing role. *Social Work Forum,* 13 (4): 7-13.

1586. Venkatesan, S., 1989, Expresssive art therapy for childhood fears: A case study. *Indian Journal of Clinical Psychology,* 16 (2): 90-92.

1587. Venkatesan, S (1990), Test Review: CIP Time Perception Scale, Indian. *Journal of Clinical Psychology,* 17 (2): 90-91

1588. Venkatesan, S. (1993) Disciplining Children: Some problems and issues. *Journal of Indian Education,* 19 (2) 9-11.

1589. Verma, I.C., JayashankaRaopa, B.S., and Palani, M., 1982, Effect of transcendental meditation on the performance of some cognitive psychological tests. *Indian Journal of Medical Research,* 71s, p 136-143.

AUTHOR INDEX

SUBJECT INDEX

APPENDIX III

LIST OF LIBRARIES AND DOCUMENTATION CENTERS

Sl.No.	Center and Address
1.	National Institute for the Mentally Handicapped Manovikasnagar, Secunderabad: 500 009
2.	Osmania Medical College, Koti, Hyderabad: 500 001
3.	Gandhi Medical College, Bashirbagh, Hyderabad: 500 003
4.	Osmania University Library, O.U.Campus; Hyderabad: 500 007
5.	College of Social Work, Red Hills, Hyderabad: 500 004
6.	Institute of Genetics, Nizamia Observatory, Ameerpet, Hyderabad: 500 012
7.	Centre for Economic and Social Sciences, Ameerpet, Hyderabad: 500 012
8.	College of Nursing, Rajbhavan Road, Hyderabad: 500 001
9.	Council for Social Development, Vidyanagar, O.U. Campus, Hyderabad: 500 007
10.	Institute of Mental Health, Erragadda, Hyderabad: 500 004
11.	National Institute for Mental Health and Neurosciences Hosur Road, Bangalore: 560029
12.	All India Institute of Speech and Hearing, Mysore, Karnataka.
13.	Kerala University, Cochin, Kerala
14.	Ali Yavar Jung National Institute for the Hearing Handicapped, Bombay, Maharastra
15.	Calcutta University, Calcutta, West Bengal
16.	PGIMR, Chandigarh, Punjab

COMPUTERISED BIBLIOGRAPHY SERVICES,CBS,

Dear Madam/Sir

This is to announce that we have started a reference search programme from our Computerised Bibliography Service (CBS), for the convenience of prospective researchers in the area of disability and impairments.

As a social scientist, you would have often encountered difficulty in searching and matching references for the proposed topic of your dissertation/thesis/research article in the area of disability and impairments. In order to overcome this difficulty and to save your precious time and energy, we have compiled a list of over one thousand five hundred articles/ research titles from over hundred Indian journal on various topics in the field of disability of impairments.

We offer consultancy services by way of posting you reference lists for any specific topic of your research/dissertation. The service charges are as follows:

Number of references listed	*Rate*
Minimum of 20 or below	Rs. 200.00
Every additional 10 references	Rs. 100.00
Postal charges	As applicable

We have access to photocopying a limited number of articles available in our data bank. The cost of photocopying per exposure is Re 0.75 paise.

The data bank of research titles on various aspects of disability and impairments has been compiled on a specially developed user friendly software, which is a modified version of FOXPRO. The software facilitates easy accessibility to available research titles as also it provides the facility for alterations/additions to existing data bank as and when needed. This software is currently priced at Rs. 5,000, (Rupees Five Thousand Only), excluding postage and handling charges.

You are welcome to use these services as per your convenience. Please mail your requests in the prescribed form.

Thanking you,

Cordially,
for Behaviour Controls Research Division

29/A, Road No. 1
West Nehru Nagar
Secunderabad-500026
Phones : 8063719, 803571

CICIL LIST

CONCEPTS IN COMMUNICATION, INFORMATICS & LIBRARIANSHIP

(CICIL)

General Editor: **S.P. AGRAWAL**

CICIL-1 Development of Library Services in India: Social Science Information
S.P. Agrawal Rs. 150

CICIL-2 Development of Documentation in India: Social Science Information
S.P. Agrawal Rs. 250

CICIL-3 UNESCO and Social Sciences: Retrospect and Prospect
S.P. Agrawal and **J.C. Aggarwal** Rs. 250

CICIL-4 INDIANA : A Bibliography of Bibliographical Sources
M.K. Jain Rs. 200

CICIL-5 Dimensions of Library and Information Science: Kaula Festschrift
V. Venkatappaiah (Eds.) Rs. 600

CICIL-6 Book Numbers: Some Indian Methods
M.P. Satija and **S.P. Agrawal** Rs. 100

CICIL-7 National Policy for University Libraries in India: Problems and Perspectives
N.B. Inamdar and **L.S. Ramaiah** (Ed.) Rs. 250

CICIL-8 Media Utilisation for the Development of Women and Children
B.S. Thakur and **Binod C. Agrawal** Rs. 150

CICIL-9 Terrorism: An Annotated Bibliography
Susheela Bhan (Ed.) Rs. 275

CICIL-10 Transnational Library Relations: The Indo-American Experience
M.B. Konnur Rs. 175

CICIL-11 Geography of Marketing and Commercial Activities in India (Documentation on Research Information)
R.S. Dixit Rs. 130

CICIL-12 Information India 1988 Global View
S.P. Agrawal and **J.C. Aggarwal** Rs. 200

CICIL-13 Women's Education in India: Historical Review, Present Status and Perspective Plan
S.P. Agrawal and **J.C. Aggarwal** Rs. 360

CICIL-14 Cultural Communication in India: Role and Impact of Phonograms
J.M. Ojha Rs. 220

CICIL-15 Second Historical Survey of Educational Development in India:

Select Documents 1985-1989
S.P. Agrawal and **J.C. Aggarwal** Rs. 490

CICIL-16 Documentation Encyclopaedia of UNESCO and Education
J.C. Aggarwal and **S.P. Agrawal** Rs. 800 (set of 2 parts)

CICIL-17 Attitude Towards Information: A Study of Post-Graduate Teachers and Researchers in Social Sciences
N.G. Satish (in press)

CICIL-18 Librarianship and Bureaucratic Organisation: A Study in the Sociology of Library Profession in India
P.K. Jayaswal Rs. 175

CICIL-19 Literature Search
K.A. Isaac Rs. 150

CICIL-20 Child Education in India: Index to Scholarly Writings in Indian Educational Journals and Newspapers since independence
S.P. Agrawal and **Naresh Kanta** Rs. 100

CICIL-21 Lok Sabha and Vidhan Sabha Elections in India 1989 & 1990: Process and Results with Comparative Study of Manifestos
S.P. Agrawal and **J.C. Aggarwal** Rs. 250

CICIL-22 Islamic Studies in India: A Survey of Human, Institutional and Documentary Sources
Mohamed Taher Rs. 180

CICIL-23 Panchayati Raj: An Annotated Bibliography
N.B. Inamdar, N.G. Satish and **Anil Takalkar** 290

CICIL-24 Information India 1989-90: Global View
S.P. Agrawal and **J.C. Aggarwal** Rs. 500

CICIL-25 First Handbook of Psychological and Social Instruments
Udai Pareek and **T. Venkateswara Rao** Rs. 500

CICIL-26 Educational and Social Uplift of Backward Classes: At What Cost and How? Mandal Commission and After
S.P. Agrawal and **J.C. Aggarwal** Rs. 275

CICIL-27 Mass Media and New Horizons: Impact of TV & Video an Urban Milieu
H.R. Trivedi Rs. 180

CICIL-28 Indian Writings on Education : An Indicator to Indian Educational Journals Grouped by Subject Deseriptors 1979 to 1986 (in two parts)
S.P. Agarwal Rs. 900 (per set)

CICIL-29 Nation in Crisis
S.P. Agrawal and **J.C. Aggarwal** Rs. 200

CICIL-30 Information India 1990-91: Global View
S.P. Agrawal and **J.C. Aggarwal** Rs. 500

CICIL-31 Development of University Libraries in India after Independence
O.P. Gupta Rs. 270

CICIL-32 Handbook on Child : With Historical Background
Pramila Pandit Barooah Rs. 320

CICIL-33 Weaker Section in Indian Society : Undiscovered Past, Uncertain Present and Unpredictable Future : Index to Writings in Indian Scholarly Journals and 10 National Newspapers Classified under 1500 Descriptors 1886-1990
S.P. Agrawal and **Rajeev Kumar Sharma** Rs. 600

CICIL-34 Communication Informatics and Librarianship in India : An Introductory Guide to Publications Based on a Survey of Libraries in Capital City of India
S.P. Agrawal and **Pushpa Rani Sharma** Rs. 720

CICIL-35 Problems of Collection Development in Special Libraries
M.S. Sridhar Rs. 225

CICIL-36 National Information Resources for Social Sciences in India : Mobilisation, Dispersal and International Enhancement
S.P. Agrawal Rs. 225

CICIL-37 Modern History of Punjab : A Look Back into Ancient Peaceful Punjab Focusing Confrontation and Failures Leading to Present Punjab Problem, and a Peep Ahead : Relevant Select Documents
J.C. Aggarwal and **S.P. Agrawal** Rs. 400

CICIL-38 India Information Sources : Economics and Business
Kyllikki Ruokonen and Manohar Lal Rs.

CICIL-39 Educational Planning in India : With a Slant to Educational Financing and Administration, Vol. 1, Reports of Committees and Commissions, Five Year Plans, Statistical Tables
J.C. Aggarwal and **S.P. Agrawal** Rs. 650

CICIL-40 Integrated Library System : Two Case Studies : Latin America and India
Maria Luiza Rigo Pasquarelli, Rosaly Favero Krzyanowski, Ines Maria M. Imperatriz and **S.P. Agrawal** Rs. 160

CICIL-41 Social Science Information in India: Effort towards Bibliographical Control
S.D. Vyas Rs. 300

CICIL-42 Higher Education in India Since Independence: U.G.C. and Its Approach
O.P. Gupta Rs. 360

CICIL-43 Government and Politics in India: A Bibliographical Study of Contemporary Scenario Chronicling Rajiv Gandhi Era
S.P. Agrawal and **Rajeev Kumar Sharma** Rs. 500

CICIL-44 Second Handbook of Psychological and Social Instruments
D.M. Pestonjee Rs. 300

CICIL-45 Development/Digression Diary of India; 3D Companion Volume to Information India: 1990-91
S.P. Agrawal Rs. 200

CICIL-46 Development/Digression Diary of India; 3D Companion Volume to Information India: 1991-92
S.P. Agrawal Rs. 300

CICIL-47 Information India 1991-92: Global View
S.P. Agrawal and **J.C. Aggarwal** Rs. 500

CICIL-48 Committees and Commissions in India 1974, A Concept's Project, Compiled by a team of professionals guided by Virender Kumar (Vol. 12) Rs. 450

CICIL-49 Committees and Commissions in India 1975, A Concept's Project, Compiled by a team of professionals guided by Virender Kumar (Vol. 13) Rs. 450

CICIL-50 Committees and Commissions in India 1976, A Concept's Project, Compiled by a team of professionals guided Virender Kumar (Vol. 14) Rs. 450

CICIL-51 Committees and Commissions in India 1977, A Concept's Project, Compiled by a team of professionals guided by Virender Kumar (Vol. 15) (in four parts) Rs. 450 each

CICIL-52 Committees and Commissions in India 1978, A Concept's Project, Compiled by a team of professionals guided by Virender Kumar (Vol. 16) (in two parts) Rs. 450 each

CICIL-53 Subject Guide to Communication, Informatics and Librarianship in India (Based on a Survey of Library Holdings in Capital City of India)
S.P. Agrawal and **Pushpa Rani Sharma** Rs. 400

CICIL-54 Restructurring of Library and Information Science Curriculum A. Tejomurty Rs. 250

CICIL-55 Committees and Commissions in India 1979, A Concept's Project, Compiled by a team of professionals guided by Virender Kumar (Vol. 17) (in two parts) Rs. 450 each

CICIL-56 Committees and Commissions in India 1980, A Concept's Project, Compiled by a team of professionals guided by Virender Kumar (Vol. 18) (in two parts) Rs. 450 each

CICIL-57 Third Historical Survey of Educational Development in India
S.P. Agrawal and **J.C. Aggarwal** Rs. 700

CICIL-58 Model Library Legislation
Velaga Venkatappaiah Rs. 400

CICIL-59 Indian Library and Information Science Literature (1990-91)
Sewa Singh Rs. 525

CICIL-60 Librarianship and Library Science in India
Mohamed Taher and **Donald Gordon Davis, Jr**. Rs. 350

CICIL-61 Comprehensive Glossary for Library & Information Science by **O.P. Gupta** Rs.300

CICIL-62 Information India : 1992-93: Global View by **S.P. Agarwal** and **J.C. Aggarwal** Rs. 500

CICIL-63 Automation Libraries and Reference Centres: With dBase III Plus by **R K Shula** Rs 250

CICIL-64 Modern History of Jammu and Kashmir by **J.C. Aggarwal** and **S.P. Agrawal** Rs 1200

CICIL-65 Library and Information Science by **Sister M. Esperanza, A.C.** Rs 250

BIBLIOGRAOHY OF QUANTITATIVE ANALYSIS

Mental Retardation

1. Abraham, A., 1990, Behaviour modification in institutionalised mentally retarded children: Case reports. *Journal of Personality and Clinical Studies,* 6 (1): 124-126.
2. Abraham, A., Mishra, H., and Kumaraih, V., 1989, Effectiveness of behaviour modification in institution based mentally retarded children. *Journal of Personality and Clinical Studies,* 5 (3): 153-160
3. Abraham, J., ChakRaoani, B., Singh, M., Kokrady, S., and Bachhawat, B.K., 1969, Hurler's disease: A clinical and biochemical study of a case. *Indian Journal of Medical Research,* 57 (9): 1761-1766.
4. Achar, S.T., and Benjamin, V., 1953, Observations on nutritional dystrophy: Clinical, pathological and biochemical aspects. *Indian Journal of Child Health,* 2 (1): 1.
5. Achar, S.T., and Thambiah, S., 1954, Pyogenic meningitis in children. *Indian Journal of Child Health,* 3 (1): 5.
6. Adiseshiah, W.T.V., 1972, Rehabilitation programme for handicapped people in Madras. *The Indian Journal of Social Work,* 33 (3): 257-268.
7. Agarwal, K.G., 1977 Mental deficiency research in India. *Indian Journal of Mental Retardation,* 10 (2): 70-87.
8. Agarwal, K.G., and Dhar, V., 1983, Causal attribution and disability. *Journal of Psychological Researches,* 32 (2): 81-86.
9. Agarwal, V.K., and Kumar, P., 1969, A follow up study of treated cases of tuberculous meningitis. *Indian Pediatrics,* 6 p 291.
10. Aggarwal, V.P., and Bharadwaj, T.P., 1973, Changes in heptatic ribonucleoproteins in kwashiorkor. *Indian Journal of Pediatrics,* 40 (300): 40.
11. Agrawal, K.G., and Gandhi, J.S. ,1968, A comparative study of